THE WORLD OF SCIENCE
WORKING WITH
COMPUTERS

THE WORLD OF SCIENCE
WORKING WITH
COMPUTERS+

KEITH WICKS

Facts On File Publications
New York, New York • Bicester, England

WORKING WITH COMPUTERS

Library of Congress Cataloging in Publication Data

Main entry under title:

World of Science

   Includes index.
   Summary: A twenty-five volume encyclopedia of
scientific subjects, designed for eight- to twelve-year-olds.
One volume is entirely devoted to projects.
   1. Science—Dictionaries, Juvenile.   1. Science—
Dictionaries
Q121.J86 1984   500   84-1654

ISBN 0-8160-1071-4

Printed in Italy
10 9 8 7 6 5 4 3 2 1

Consultant editors
Eleanor Felder, Former Managing Editor, **New Book of
Knowledge**
James Neujahr, Dean of the School of Education, City
College of New York
Ethan Signer, Professor of Biology, Massachusetts
Institute of Technology
J. Tuzo Wilson, Director General, Ontario Science Centre

Previous pages
The computer is an
important aid for
designers in many
industries. Here an
engineer uses computer
graphics to experiment
with the design of a
streamlined car.

Editor Penny Clarke
Designer Roger Kohn

CONTENTS

INTRODUCTION

omises, promises   **6**
ng a computer   **8**
ide the computer   **10**
al instructions   **14**
nning the program   **15**
er friendliness   **16**

ENTERTAINING COMPUTERS

e computer plays games   **18**
most real   **21**

WORDS, PICTURES AND USIC

e word machine   **24**
ppling with graphics   **28**
phics made easy   **32**
king music   **36**

COMMUNICATING ITH COMPUTERS

king computers   **40**
ech synthesis   **41**
ech recognition   **43**
mmunicating by computer   **44**
abases   **47**
mmunicating for fun   **48**
ping the handicapped   **50**

COMPUTERS IN SHOPS ND FACTORIES

ind the counter   **52**
ots   **54**
robot arm   **54**
ots on the move   **60**

ssary   **62**
ex   **64**

◄The latest space game draws an enthusiastic audience at a computer fair.

◄Home computers are becoming more versatile. You can now add laser disks and video graphics components to many of them.

Note There are some unusual words in this book. They are explained in the Glossary on pages 62–63. The first time each word is used in the text it is printed in *italics*.

PROMISES, PROMISES

►Do you like hang gliding, sailing, or golf? Whatever your field of interest, the computer will enable you to enjoy it without leaving your home. Well, maybe!

►The chart shows the dramatic drop in prices that caused the home computer boom in the early 1980s. The models shown are the cheapest computers available with at least 16 *Kbytes* of RAM (Random Access Memory) built in. One Kbyte is equal to 1024 bytes.

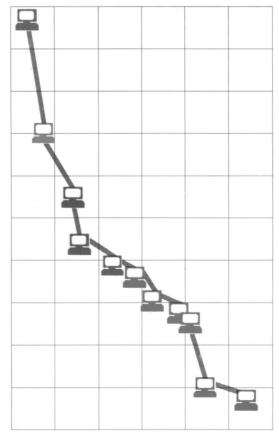

In recent years fortunes have been mad and lost through the sudden boom and crash in microcomputer sales. Once the price of a home computer had dropped t about the price of a TV set, thousands c people flocked to buy one. But now the boom is over, and computers lie forgott in cupboards in many homes. And, in some offices, microcomputers that were expected to solve all the problems of the company have hardly ever been used. Y elsewhere, computers are hard at work performing a vast range of tasks.

The boom

The firms that made the first home microcomputers did very well, although these machines were too expensive for most people. However, many other computer companies were soon formed, and they got people to buy their machi by cutting prices and by persuasive advertisements. A home computer will entertain, inform and educate you. It w solve your problems, carry out boring

Helps with homework

Useful for letters

▲ A home micro can fulfil these promises. But beware of the problems. You may need to buy other things besides the computer to make a system that does what you want.

Helps understand science

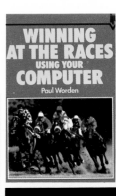
Plays games and entertains

ks and leave you with more time to oy yourself. At least, that is what the nufacturers said.

The public were greatly impressed, and nputer sales rose rapidly. By 1981, the m was well under way, and was soon king fortunes for many in the nputer industry.

e crash

1984 the boom had ended, and more tunes were being lost than were being de in the computer industry. Firms t refused to cut their prices found that ir sales quickly declined. And firms t did cut their prices found that their ofits were too low to pay their staff and ppliers. Also, once people had bought a nputer, there was a problem in 'suading them to buy another. Many isfied customers did not want to change another computer, even if it was pposed to be better. And people appointed with their first purchase did want to risk further disappointment.

e problems

e main reason for disappointment was t many people expected too much for little. Computers can usually do what ir makers claim. But you may have to nd a lot of money on extra items in er to use a computer in exactly the y you want. Or you may have to spend ot of time finding out why things are ng wrong.

The following pages cover many of the ks that computers can perform, various

items of additional equipment, and some of the problems that can arise. Understanding what computers can do will help to avoid disappointment when you decide to get a computer to work for you.

◄ Some people hope that their home computer will help them make their fortune at gambling. These books tell you how to select horses and football teams using your computer. But have you heard of anyone who has made

their fortune as a result? At best, such methods may help people to lose their money more slowly.

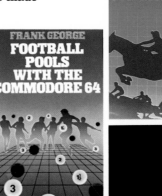

▲Some colleges encourage all their students to use computers, no matter taking. Instead of having to visit the library, a student can obtain a great deal of screen, simply by pressing a few buttons. Some systems show who is working at each building and allow y to contact anyone fo help or discussion.

…most everybody should find it easy to
… a computer. You do not need to
…derstand how the computer works, and
…do not need any knowledge of
…thematics.

…me computer equipment

…e simplest home computer system
…sists of three main units: computer,
…sette recorder and TV set. This, and
…y other equipment used for computing
…alled the *hardware*. Most people who
…nt a home computer already have a
…sette recorder and TV set, so the
…nputer and a few connecting leads are
… that are needed to form a complete
…nputer system.

…eparing for action

…fore a computer can carry out any task,
…nust receive a set of instructions called
…program. This is also called *software*,
…d is what determines whether the
…nputer acts as a games machine, or
…ries out some other task, such as
…wing diagrams, or making music. For
…ome computer, the program usually
…sists of coded signals recorded on a
…sette tape. They sound like whistles or
… unpleasant buzz. The tape is played on
…assette machine connected to the
…nputer. As a result, the instructions
…ter the computer as a stream of
…ctrical signals. These are held, or
…red, in a part of the computer called
… *memory*.

…The computer is now ready for action,
…d details of what to do next will
…bably appear on the screen. You may
have to press buttons on the keyboard, or
operate some other device connected to
the computer.

Operating a computer, therefore,
involves three main steps: connecting the
equipment together; loading a program
into the computer; and following
instructions that are supplied with the
program, or that appear on the screen.
Most games and other popular programs
are simple to use – if they were difficult,
they would not be popular and so would
not be profitable for the makers.

Other hardware

Computers used for business purposes,
and many home computers, use a
magnetic *disk* unit instead of a cassette
machine, and a special monitor screen
instead of a TV set. The disk unit and
screen may be built in to the computer, or
supplied separately. These refinements
make the computer system even easier to
use. Many other items of hardware can be
connected to the system. For example, a
joystick unit makes it easier to play some
games. And a printer will be essential for
word processing.

…Iost business
…tems use magnetic
…ks instead of
…settes to store
…grams and
…ormation. In the
…tem shown here, the
…ks are inserted in
… slots on the right-
…d side of the
…nitor. The printer is
…d mostly for letters
…other documents.

▲Disk units are
available for most
home computers. This
unit takes disks
measuring 5¼ in across.

INSIDE THE COMPUTER

Most home computers look quite simple, consisting of a shallow plastic box with a keyboard on top. Yet inside are electronic circuits much more complex than those in a TV set. You cannot see just how complex the circuits are because they are mostly concealed within tiny components called integrated circuits. These are often called silicon chips, as the microscopic circuits are formed on slices of silicon crystal.

Chips

Hundreds, or even thousands, of transistors and other components may be formed on a single *chip*. But all you can see is the plastic or ceramic block that protects the circuit, and two rows of metal legs for connecting the chip to other parts in the computer.

The most important chip is called the *microprocessor*. This controls the whole operation of the computer. Some chips receive signals from input devices, such as the keyboard or a joystick. And other chips send signals to output devices, such as the screen, or a printer.

Another important group of chips form the computer's memory – the place where it stores information, and instructions on what to do with the information.

Bits and bytes

Whatever task a computer performs, it has to handle some kind of information. This may be the numbers in a calculation, details of a picture on the screen or the words in a document. The information in the computer is in the form of a simple code. In most home computers, the code word consists of eight parts. More elaborate machines use a 16-part or 32-part code. The code is called *binary*, which means that each part has two possible values. Instructions that tell the computer what to do are coded in this way too.

On paper, we represent these values using the digits 0 and 1. For example, the code 01001011 may represent the letter K. The numbers 0 and 1 are known as *bits*, which is short for binary digits. And the group of eight bits is called a *byte*. As each of the eight bits can be 0 or 1, there

are 256 possible combinations, ranging from 00000000 to 11111111. So there are ample codes to represent all the letters of the alphabet, punctuation marks, symbols, numerals and other items.

In the computer, each bit is represent by the presence (1) or absence (0) of a small, fixed voltage. The eight-bit volta, patterns thus formed are stored in the computer's memory chips.

Memories

There are two main types of memory in the computer *ROM* and *RAM*. They bot consist of chips containing circuits designed to store thousands of bytes of

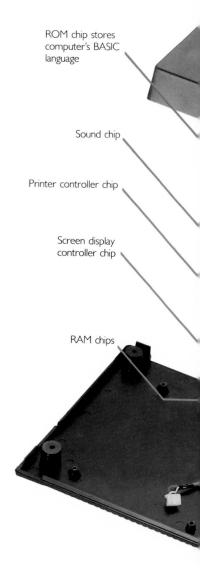

ROM chip stores computer's BASIC language

Sound chip

Printer controller chip

Screen display controller chip

RAM chips

▲Inside the Amstrad CPC 6128, an advanced home microcomputer.

ormation or instructions.

The ROM, or Read Only Memory, acts her like a printed book. It contains rmanent information needed by the mputer to carry out its tasks. This is ad (obtained) by the computer whenever cessary.

The RAM is a Read And write Memory, re usually called a Random Access emory. This part of the memory acts as electronic notebook. It is a temporary re of information and instructions, ich you can remove or change as you

like. In other words, besides reading the contents of the RAM, you can also write (put) new coded instructions into it.

When you switch on the computer, a large part of the RAM is empty. When you load a program into the computer from a cassette or disk, the instructions contained in the program are changed into electrical signals and stored in the RAM. If you later load another program into the computer, this will replace the original program stored in the RAM, so that the computer can carry out a different task. On switching off, anything stored in the RAM is lost. So a program must be loaded in again the next time that the computer is used.

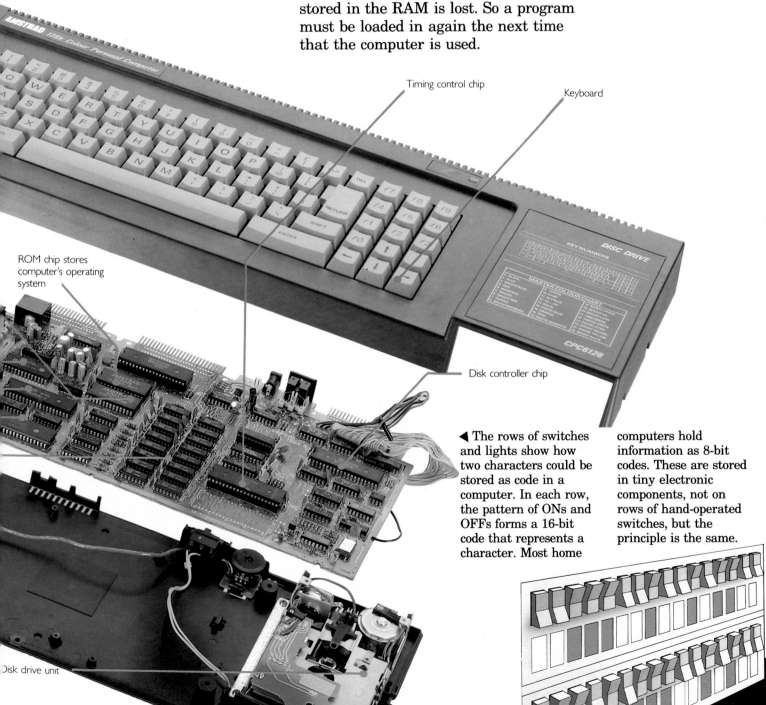

Timing control chip

Keyboard

ROM chip stores computer's operating system

Disk controller chip

Disk drive unit

◀ The rows of switches and lights show how two characters could be stored as code in a computer. In each row, the pattern of ONs and OFFs forms a 16-bit code that represents a character. Most home computers hold information as 8-bit codes. These are stored in tiny electronic components, not on rows of hand-operated switches, but the principle is the same.

11

The micropr
chip is the c
centre of the
This highly
photograph

VITAL INSTRUCTIONS

You can use a computer as a simple electronic calculator without having to load a program into its memory. This is an example of using the computer in what is called direct mode. But a program is necessary if you are to make full use of the computer's power.

Basic examples

Any instructions that you give the computer must be in a language that the computer can understand. Most microcomputers understand a language called *BASIC* – Beginners' All-purpose Symbolic Instruction Code. There are many varieties of this language, but they all have much in common. BASIC is made up of various English words, letters, numbers and symbols.

On a calculator, if you punch in 5+4=, the answer 9 will appear. But not so on the computer. You have to type in PRINT 5+4 and then press a key marked RETURN or ENTER. The answer should then appear on the screen. But, in BASIC, instead of 5×4, you would use 5*4 on the computer. And 5/4 would be used instead of 5÷4. These are simple examples of using BASIC language. Other simple commands in BASIC will enable you to

▼This computer has slots to take plug-in program cartridges. The programs are stored on ROM chips inside the cartridges. Programs on cartridges are ready to use almost immediately, whereas it may take many minutes to load in a program recorded on tape.

▼Unlike other home computers, the Jupiter Ace had the FORTH language built in instead of the usual BASIC. FORTH is especially useful for

controlling moveme⟨ This language was developed originally enable a computer ⟨ position a radio telescope.

work out more complex mathematical problems on the screen.

Now suppose that you wanted to change some temperatures in Celsius t⟨ Fahrenheit. The formula for the conversion is:

$$\text{Fahrenheit} = \text{Celsius} \times 9 \div 5 + 32$$

So, to convert 20°C, you could type in:

PRINT 20*9/5+32

On pressing the RETURN or ENTER k⟨ the answer 68 would appear on the screen.

It is often very useful to be able to perform quick calculations like this in direct mode. But suppose that you wan⟨ to make up a table to convert all the temperatures from 1° to 200° Celsius in⟨ Fahrenheit. Entering all these figures i⟨ direct mode would take a long time. A much better approach would be to load ⟨ suitable program into the computer. Programs for converting various kinds ⟨ measurements can be purchased. But it⟨

RUNNING THE PROGRAM

easy to write them yourself, once you
e learnt the rules of BASIC. The
wing BASIC program will perform the
perature conversions automatically.
ply type it in on the keyboard,
embering to press the RETURN or
TER key at the end of each line.

```
10  FOR C = 1 TO 200
20  F = C*9/5+32
30  PRINT C,F
40  NEXT C
```

otice that each line must be
bered. The actual numbers used are
important, so long as they increase
one line to the next. However, it is
al to leave gaps in the numbering.
makes it easy to add extra lines
r, if it is necessary – and it often is.

Once the program has been typed in, it
can be stored on a cassette tape (or disk)
and kept for future use. To use the
program immediately, simply type in
RUN. You should see the Celsius
temperatures from 1 to 200, with their
Fahrenheit equivalents, appear rapidly
down the screen. A typical microcomputer
takes under 30 seconds to perform the
calculations and display them on the
screen.

Although we have not yet dealt with all
the BASIC *commands* used in this
program, you may already have guessed
how the program works. Line 10 simply
means that we will use the letter C to
represent the numbers from 1 to 200,
starting at 1. These are the Celsius
temperatures that we want to convert.
The letter C is used as it is easy to
remember that it stands for Celsius, but
another letter could be used instead. In
line 20 we use F to represent the
Fahrenheit temperature, and state how
the computer is to calculate it from the
Celsius temperature. Line 30 causes the
first value of C, which is 1, to be
displayed, followed by the calculated
value of F. The comma between C and F
in this line ensures that a space will
appear between the two figures – another
feature of BASIC. Line 40 then calls for
the process to be repeated using the next
value of C, which is 2, and so on. When
the last value of C (200) has been dealt
with, the program will stop running.

◄Programs are
available to make
popular computers run
on other languages
besides BASIC. The

FORTH program
cassettes shown here
are for the Commodore
64 and Spectrum home
computers.

)GO is a computer
uage widely used
hools, as it is ideal
aching the
ciples of
uting. LOGO is
demonstrated by
g it to control a
le robot called a

floor turtle. The three
LOGO programs in the
picture are a disk
version for the
Commodore 64, a tape
cassette version for the
Spectrum, and a
cartridge for the Atari.

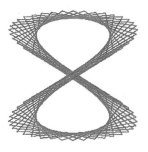

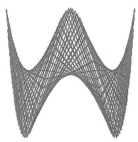

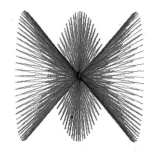

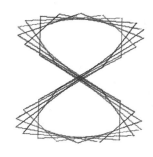

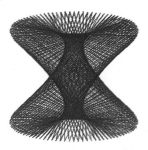

▲These repetitive line
drawings were made
on a computer screen
using commands in
LOGO language.

USER FRIENDLINESS

The example of the temperature conversion shows how, with a simple program, the computer can perform useful tasks quickly. But this program has many weaknesses. Computer users would say that it is an unfriendly program. For example, every time it is run on the computer, it will perform the same calculations. To get it to convert other temperatures, the figures in line 10 would have to be altered. This is easy if the person using the computer understands how to program in BASIC, but impossible if not.

A better approach is to design the program so that the user is asked to type in the required temperature range on the screen.

Easier to read
Another problem is that the figures will appear so fast that there is no time to read them before they have moved off the top of the screen to make room for the next figures to appear at the bottom. To overcome this, the program could be made to pause when a screenful of information is displayed, and continue only when you press one of the keys. To make this clear to the person using the computer, the program could print a message at the bottom of the screen saying: 'Press any key to continue'.

Extra facilities
It might be necessary at some time to convert Fahrenheit temperatures to Celsius. This facility could easily be added. At the start, a question would appear on the screen, asking the user to press one of two keys, according to which

type of conversion is required.

As the object is to produce a temperature conversion table, it would obviously be sensible to connect a print to the computer and get the informatio printed automatically. Besides saving time in copying the information from tl screen, this also avoids errors. The computer could ask the user to press th 'P' key to get the results on the printer the 'S' key to get the results on the scre if a printer is not available.

Of course, it takes time to learn how write good programs. But it is not difficult. A good program should provid every facility that the user might want yet be extremely easy to use. Programs like this are described as being user friendly.

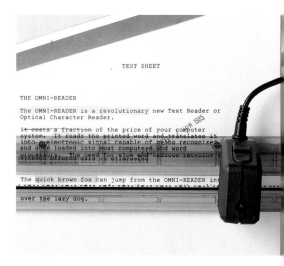

▲Extra equipment can make a computer system more user friendly. If you want to store text in a computer, you usually have to type it all on the keyboard. However, if the words are already in typed form, the Omni-reader enables them to be fed quickly into the computer line by line. A reading device is slid across each line of text in turn. From the images of the letters, it forms electronic signals, which are fed into the computer.

►Apple's Lisa was designed to be more user friendly than other computers. Various features of Lisa are shown arou the edges of the scre as symbols called ic The small box, calle mouse, is moved ov the table by hand. makes a small arro move about the scre To select the feature required, the arrow positioned over the symbol, and a butto pressed. This is mu easier than typing commands on the keyboard.

ENTERTAINING COMPUTERS

►Space Invaders became a popular arcade game in the late 1970s. Like many other arcade games, it can now be played on home computers too.

We usually think of computer games being played in amusement arcades or on cheap home computers. But the first computer games were played on powerful *mainframe* computers in the late 1950s. These computers were designed for serious tasks, such as data processing. But the technicians running them enjoyed the challenge of trying to make them do something more entertaining. The most notable of the early computer games was developed by Martin Graetz and others at the Massachusetts Institute of Technology, in the USA. The year was 1962, and the name of the game was Spacewar. Playing Spacewar quickly became a craze among the students, and people who wanted to do work on the computers often complained that they had been taken over by the games players.

In those days, computers were too expensive to be sold just for playing

games, and it was not until the 1970s that computer games went on sale in shops and stores.

Pong
In 1972, a game called Pong appeared a bar in Sunnyvale, California. The inventor was a local man named Nolan Bushnell. Pong was an electronic versi of table tennis, with simple *graphics* o black-and-white screen. A central line represented the net, and the ball was a small blob. A short line at each end of screen represented the two players' bat Controls on the machine allowed the players to move their bats, the object being to hit the ball past their opponer

The Pong machine was a simple computer, permanently programmed to play that game. It moved the ball acro the screen and checked to see if the player's bat was correctly positioned w

olan Bushnell,
ntor of the
puter game Pong,
and founder of the
Atari Corporation.

Invaders from Japan

In 1978, Space Invaders came to the United States from Japan. The game was a sensation in arcades. The public, it seemed, liked nothing better than zapping aliens. At this time, home computers were appearing in the stores, but were too expensive for most people. The manufacturers were quick to realize that they would sell more machines if people could play Space Invaders and similar games on them. Within a few years, the production of games programs had become a massive new industry.

ball arrived at the far end. If so, then
ball was made to move back to the
er end, just as if it had bounced from a
l bat. If the bat was not in the right
ition, then the ball would not be
urned, and the player who had just hit
ball would be awarded a point. The
y would then continue, the winner
ng the player with the most points at
end. By modern standards, the
phics were extremely crude. But it was
npletely new and an instant success.

A fantasy world

One of the most popular kinds of computer game is the adventure. The player usually has a task such as finding a treasure, solving a crime or destroying an enemy. The action may take place in outer space, a maze, a system of underground caves, or some strange and fantastic land.

Part of the fun of these games is that it often takes many weeks to complete an adventure game. Because of this, when you want to stop, you can usually store your position on tape. The next time you want to play, the stored information is loaded back into the computer. The game

◄Modern versions of space war games use complex graphics. Now that memory chips are relatively cheap, even home computers can store all the information needed to produce graphics like this.

▲Even a cheap home computer system will enable you to enjoy some of the best adventure games programs.

►Valhalla is an adventure game with pictures and text. The player has to find the way to Valhalla and overcome problems that arise by typing commands at the bottom of the screen.

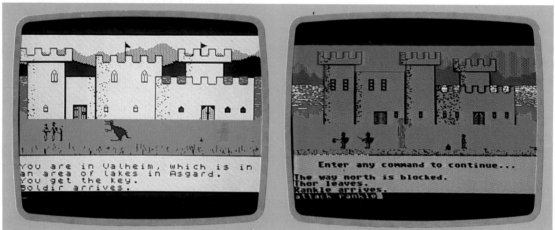

►When playing an adventure game, you see only one part of the location at a time. So it may help to draw a map on paper as you make your journey – otherwise you may end up back where you started. The large picture shows what a completed map might look like. The small picture shows one of the 25 separate screen displays that make up the map.

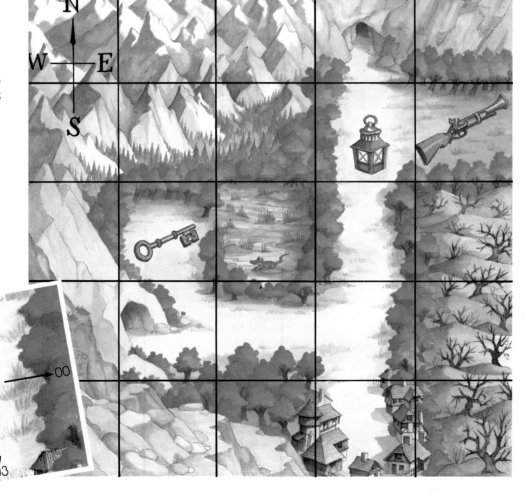

LMOST REAL

ead of putting the player in a fantasy
ld, some games programs do the
osite. They copy, or simulate, real-life
its, such as a ball game or chess, or
e hazardous occupations, such as
nd Prix racing or aerobatics.

puter *simulations* also have serious
s. For example, aircraft pilots undergo
ial training using computer-controlled
ipment. This simulates the way real
raft would respond to the controls.

ulation for fun

early arcade game of Pong was a
ple example of simulation. The image
he screen was a crude picture of a
e tennis table, with a net, two bats
a ball. By comparison, some games
ved on today's home computers are
erb. Instead of a picture where
rything looks flat, the best programs
w a perspective view. Objects that are
posed to be farther from you are
ller, thus giving an impression of
th. For this reason, such images are
etimes wrongly described as three-
ensional, or 3-D, graphics.

true 3-D graphics, the images appear
e really solid, with some parts behind,
n front of, the screen. The effect is an
sion produced when two slightly
erent coloured images are viewed
ugh a pair of glasses with different
ured filters. This technique has been
d in a few educational programs to
w clearly some of the shapes studied
olid geometry. But the filters
l the look of most colours on the
en and it is a nuisance having to wear
sses, so true depth is rarely simulated
the screen.

owever, a very important use of
puters is to create pairs of printed
ures which, when viewed together,
e a true 3-D image of an object.
ntists use this technique to show the
pes of complex molecules.

ultimate reality

ne games graphics are now so good
t they resemble a cartoon-style film.
at attention is paid to detail. For
mple, besides seeing a ball sailing

through the air, you also see its shadow
on the ground.

With graphics looking like a cartoon,
the games player at the computer controls
is acting almost as a film director.
Eventually, it will become possible to
make the players on screen look like
anyone you want. So you will be able to
show yourself playing with top stars.

The sounds that accompany some
computer games are also quite realistic,
and it cannot be long before all the
characters that appear on screen will be
able to talk.

▼Any game
traditionally played on
a board can be
simulated on a
computer. The game
being played here is
backgammon. The
player has to indicate
which counters to move
by typing on the
keyboard. Then the
computer will take its
turn.

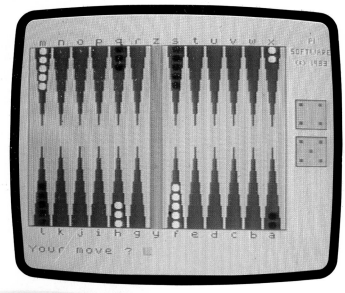

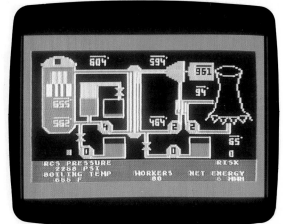

◀Dangerous
experiments can be
safely simulated. This
educational program
by Atari enables you to
try running a nuclear
power station.

▶Scientists used
graphics to form this
image of a complex
DNA molecule on
the screen of a
powerful computer.
The image can be
turned around to
show details hidden
in the view shown
here. The numbers
indicate the parts of
the molecule.

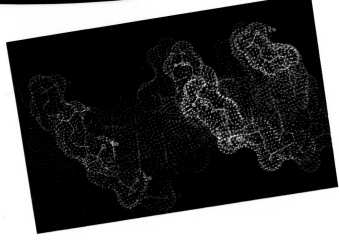

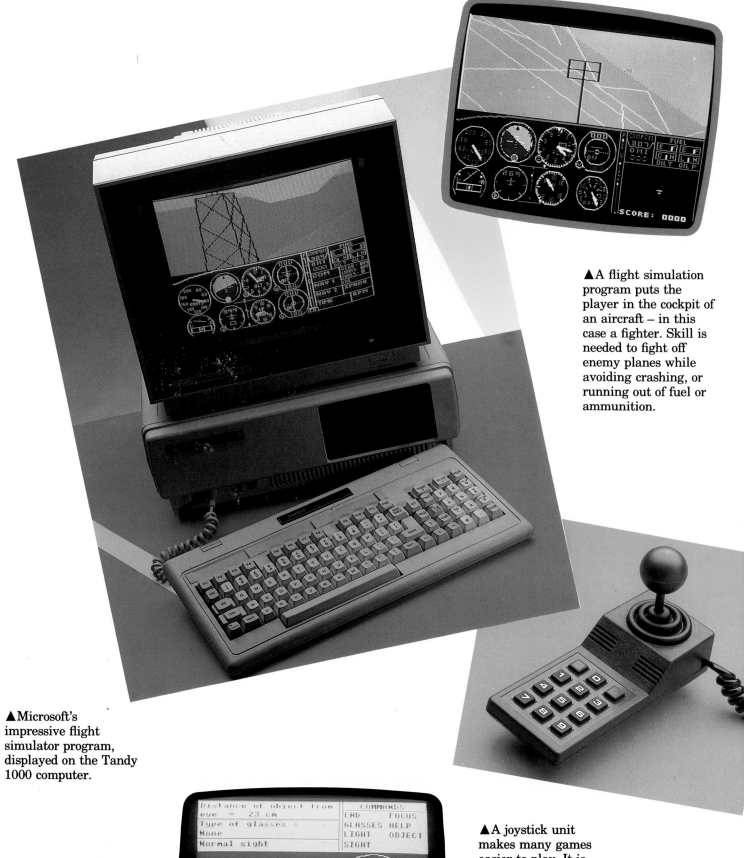

▲A flight simulation program puts the player in the cockpit of an aircraft – in this case a fighter. Skill is needed to fight off enemy planes while avoiding crashing, or running out of fuel or ammunition.

▲Microsoft's impressive flight simulator program, displayed on the Tandy 1000 computer.

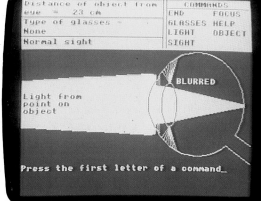

▲A joystick unit makes many games easier to play. It is especially useful in simulation games, because it makes the player feel in control of a vehicle or other moving object.

►This simulation program demonstrates how our eyes work. It shows what causes some people to see blurred images. And you can experiment with various types of spectacle lens to try improving the image.

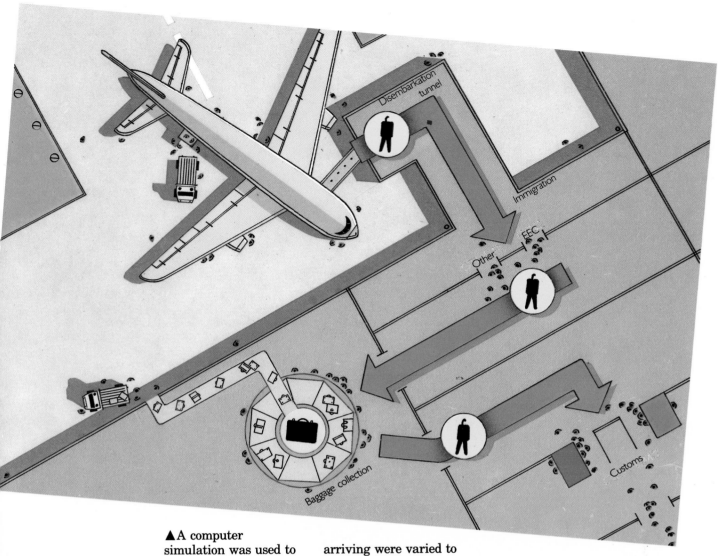

▲A computer simulation was used to help design a new terminal at London's Heathrow Airport. The numbers of aircraft and passengers arriving were varied to see what baggage, customs and immigration services would be needed at various times.

◄Pilots are trained on computer-controlled flight simulators. The trainees operate real aircraft controls and see a simulation of the view from the cabin. To make the experience as realistic as possible, the motion of the aircraft is simulated too. The platform supporting the simulator is tilted in various directions by the pistons below.

3 WORDS, PICTURES AND MUSIC

THE WORD MACHINE

Words typed on an ordinary typewriter are printed immediately on the paper. With a word processing system, the words appear first on the screen. If you want to alter some words, or the way a document is arranged, you can change the text o its layout on the screen. When this ha been done, the text can be printed on paper or saved (stored) on a magnetic disk.

▼A portable computer allows word processing to be done while travelling.

Convenience and perfection

At any time, you can load text stored disk back into the computer for editing (alteration) or printing. Besides deletir or changing individual characters and words, whole paragraphs can be remov or transferred to another part of a document. Or they can be stored separately and inserted into another document at a later date.

These, and the many other features word processor, enable even the worst typist to produce perfect letters, neatly laid out on the paper. The word proces also makes typing faster. You do not w about making mistakes as you know tl they can be easily corrected. The write

▶After initial popularity, the Osborne computer (top left) went out of fashion when smaller portables became available. Although easily portable, the Epsom HX-20 (top right) is a versatile computer. The Sharp PC1251 (bottom right) has a small, built-in printer. Unlike the other three computers, the Casio FX700P (bottom left) has no tape or disk system of its own. A separate cassette machine must be connected.

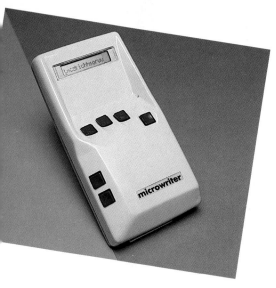

is made easier too. Ideas can be
...d in straight away, and the grammar
...ed up later on. To remind you of other
...gs you want to write, you could type
...rief notes and delete them at the end.

...d processing equipment

...t word processors used at home
...ist of a computer system with a word
...essing program. Similar systems are
...d in many offices. But, in some cases,
...dicated word processor is used. This
...ly means that the machine is
...gned to do only word processing –
...ke an ordinary microcomputer, which
...do many other things too.

...hen a microcomputer is used for word
...essing, an ordinary TV set is
...itable for reading what you have
...d. The characters on the screen are
...quite clear enough to read easily, so
...train and mistakes often occur. A
...ially designed display unit called a
...itor gives a clearer picture. The best
...itors are monochrome (single-colour)
...s, as these give a much sharper image
...n full-colour monitors.

...n ordinary cassette machine is of little
...for storing text because it is too slow.
...uld take five minutes or more to save
...ad a page of text – a great waste of
...e if you need to do this quite often.
...example, you may want to glance at
...ral documents that you have already
...ed. Clearly, a much faster storage
...em is needed for serious word
...essing. The most popular solution is
...se a disk drive. This should store or
...d a page of text in just a few seconds.
...lthough any text stored on disk can be
...layed on the screen, most people need

◄The Microwriter is a portable word processor about the size of a hand. Letters and numerals are entered by pressing various combinations of the six keys. The stored text can be transferred to an ordinary word processor and added to other material. Or a printer can be connected to get hard copy – words on paper.

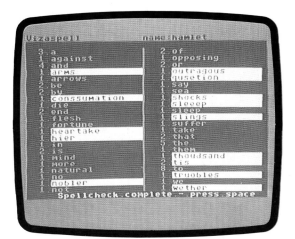

◄A speech from *Hamlet*, a play by William Shakespeare and one of Laurence Olivier's most famous roles (**bottom**), has been typed using the Vizawrite word processor. Have you spotted all the spelling mistakes? One way to make sure is to use a program for checking the spelling.

The second picture shows how the Vizaspell program checks the spelling. It lists all words and shows how many times they have been used. And it searches for these words in a stored list of common words. Any that it does not find are shown on a white background. These may be mistakes, or simply uncommon words that have not been stored. Any mistakes can be corrected before printing.

hard copy – text printed on paper. Several kinds of printer are available for this purpose.

Daisy wheel printers
The *daisy wheel* and *dot matrix* printers are the two main types used with microcomputers. A daisy wheel printer works in a similar way to an ordinary typewriter. Castings of the letters, numbers, punctuation marks and other characters are made to strike an inked ribbon, which marks the paper. These characters are fixed to the ends of flexible arms, which radiate from a central disc. The whole arrangement resembles the

▼The daisy wheel printer gives the best result, but is usually much slower than other printers.

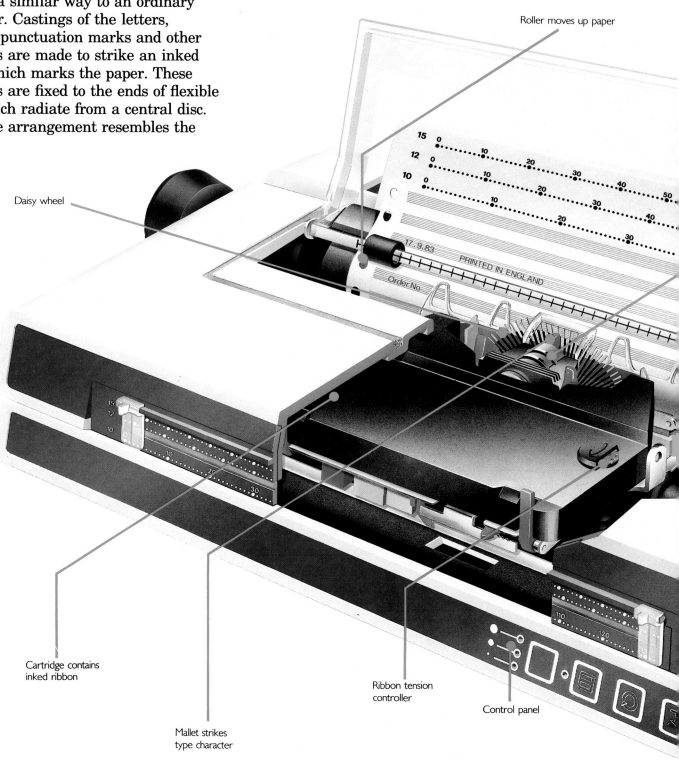

Roller moves up paper

Daisy wheel

Cartridge contains inked ribbon

Mallet strikes type character

Ribbon tension controller

Control panel

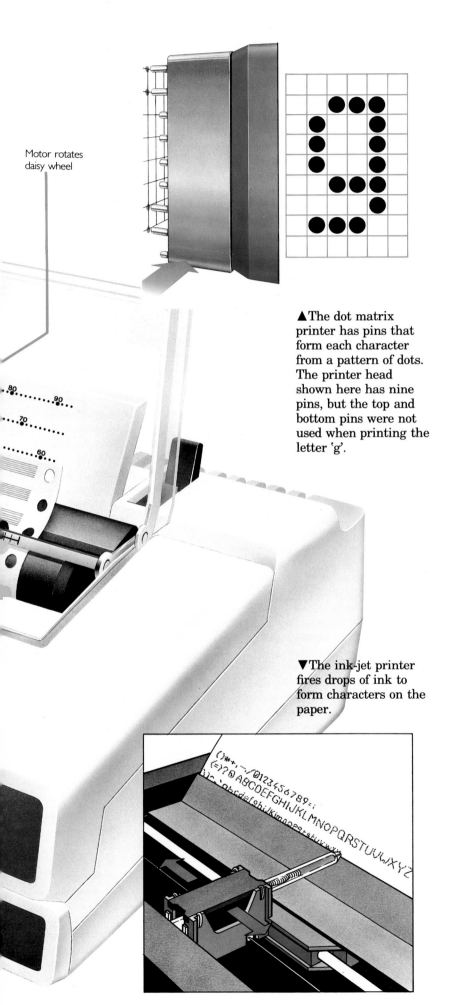

Motor rotates
daisy wheel

▲The dot matrix
printer has pins that
form each character
from a pattern of dots.
The printer head
shown here has nine
pins, but the top and
bottom pins were not
used when printing the
letter 'g'.

▼The ink-jet printer
fires drops of ink to
form characters on the
paper.

petals radiating from the centre of a
flower, hence the name daisy wheel. The
disc spins to bring the required character
in front of a metal rod, or mallet. The rod
then hits the character, so that it moves
forward and prints through the ribbon.

The daisy wheel machine gives top
quality printing, and the wheel can be
replaced when it eventually shows signs
of wear. It can also be changed if you
want a different style or size of type, or a
foreign alphabet with accents. Special
wheels are available for printing
mathematical symbols.

Dot matrix printers

A dot matrix printer forms each character
from a pattern, or matrix, of dots. If you
look closely, you may be able to see the
individual dots in the characters. The
most common type of dot matrix printer
has a column of needle-like rods that
move across the paper. Various
combinations of needles strike a ribbon to
print the dots on plain paper.

A cheap dot matrix printer might form
characters up to seven dots high and six
dots wide. In such cases, the dot pattern is
easily seen, and some words may be
slightly difficult to read. On some more
expensive dot matrix printers, the gaps
between the original dots are filled in
with more dots, formed by the same
needles. Other printers use many more
needles and form each character from a
large number of dots. The print quality of
the best dot matrix printers is almost as
good as that obtained on a daisy wheel
machine.

The advantage of using a dot matrix
printer is that it can be made to print
characters not found on any daisy wheel.
Such characters are formed by using
special commands in the computer
program to control the dot formation. As
any combination of dots can be formed,
this kind of machine is suitable for
printing graphs and diagrams.

The cheapest dot matrix printers use
heat or an electric current to mark special
paper. As the paper is fairly expensive,
anyone who needs to do a lot of printing
would be better off getting a more
expensive printer that uses ordinary plain
paper.

►Highly detailed computer graphics show an engineer the shape of a machine part.

Some scenes shown in modern films are created entirely by powerful computers. These images may be used for special effects and look deliberately artificial. Or they may look so real that you do not realize that a computer has been used. Computer graphics are used in many other ways by designers, artists, scientists and engineers. A common technique is to use the computer to show what an object looks like when viewed from any angle. The computer uses information about the object's shape to form the required view automatically. Architects, for example, can see what a new building would look like from the street. And they can see what effect various changes to the design would have, simply by changing the information in the computer.

Many home computers now have impressive graphics aids, which makes them even more appealing as games machines. But it will be a long time before they can form entirely realistic images.

▼A user-defined character representing a man.

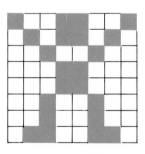

▼Complex images can be formed from groups of user-defined characters.

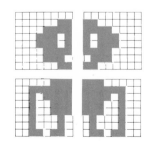

...ple graphics

...some computers the only way to form
...ures on the screen is to use special
...racters called block graphics. These
...racters each occupy the same space on
... screen as a letter or numeral. And
...y are formed in the same way too. If
... look closely at any character
...layed on the screen, you will see that
... formed from an arrangement of dots.
... typical computer, there are eight
...s of eight dots available to form each
...racter.

... block graphics, the dots make up
...izontal and vertical lines, squares,
...angles and various other shapes and
...terns. Simple diagrams and pictures
... be formed from various combinations
...hese standard arrangements of dots.
...any computers allow you to design
...r graphics blocks from any possible
...angement of dots. Such blocks are
...ed user-defined characters. They
...ble you to draw shapes that would be
...ossible to obtain with the standard set
...lock graphics characters.

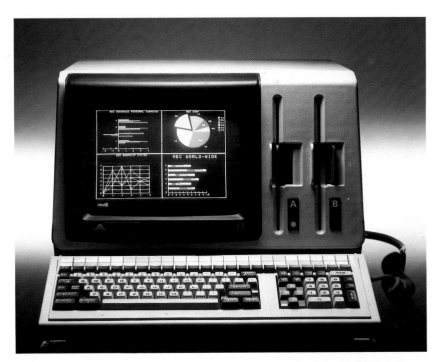

▲Microcomputers can
make groups of figures
easier to understand by
presenting them as
graphs and diagrams.

▲Once the shape of
an object has been
stored in a computer,
various views of it can
be shown on the
screen. The images
shown here were
produced using Psion's
VU-3D program on a
Spectrum home
computer. Shading has
been added to the last
image in the series.

Sprites

The best computer graphics are produced using larger groups of dots called *sprites*. On the Commodore 64 computer, for example, there are 21 rows of 24 dots available for each sprite. With so many dots available, you can design quite complex sprites. Similar images could be obtained using several user-defined characters, but there are important advantages in using sprites when images have to move across the screen.

▼Sprites are versatile graphics images that can appear to pass in front of, or behind, other sprites when they move. Here, th spacemen sprites appear to be in the foreground, and the stars in the background.

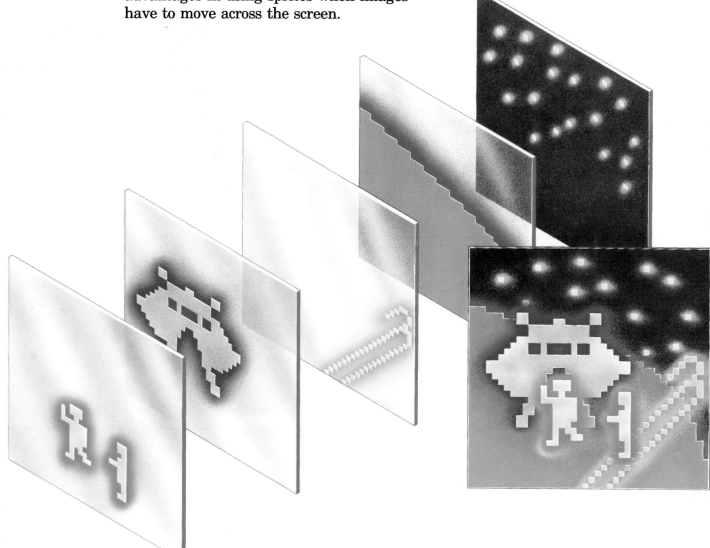

Animation

Animation is the making of moving images. On a computer, animation involves printing an image on the screen, removing it, and then printing a similar or identical image in a slightly different position. If this is done several times in very quick succession, it looks as if there is just one image moving on the screen.

In some computers user-defined characters and standard block graphics are limited in the way that they can move. Like letters and numerals, they be moved across or down the screen in steps equal to the size of one character distance equal to eight dots. This can make their movements look jerky, especially at slow speeds. But sprites ca be moved by a distance of just one dot a time. So smooth movement is possible at any speed.

Sprites have another major advantage
[in] animation. When one sprite moves to a
[par]t of the screen occupied by another
[spr]ite, the first one may appear to pass in
[fro]nt of, or behind, the other. Numbers
[giv]en to the sprites determine which one
[app]ears in front. In the system used in
[the] Commodore 64, the sprites can be
[nu]mbered from 0 to 7. If two sprites are
[pos]itioned in the same part of the screen,
[the] one with the lower number
[det]ermines the screen image. It therefore
[app]ears to be in front of the other sprite.
[Spr]ites thus help to make moving images
[mo]re realistic. Watching the best home
[com]puter graphics can be almost like
[wat]ching a cartoon film on television.

▲Fast-moving detailed
graphics, once seen
only in powerful arcade
machines, are now
possible on many home
computers.

◄This is a shot from
the film *Road to Point
Reyes*. The hills and
mountains in the
background were
produced by means of
the latest computer
graphics techniques.

31

GRAPHICS MADE EASY

Like everything else that a computer does, the formation of graphics is controlled by commands in a program. With block graphics it is easy to write a simple program that prints various blocks on the screen to build up a fixed image. With user-defined characters, sprites and animation, the task is more difficult. Of course, if you are interested mainly in using the computer, and not in programming, the answer is to buy programs with good graphics, load them into the computer and enjoy the results. However, there are various programs and devices that make it easier to produce your own graphics.

Programming aids
If you are writing a program with graphics, the sprites are usually designed first on graph paper, each square representing a dot. Then some arithmetic

is involved in order to convert the required pattern of dots into a series of numbers to feed into the computer. But programs are available to make it much easier to design the sprites. Any program that helps with some task performed on the computer is called a utility. In this particular case, a suitable utility program would enable you to design the sprites the screen by showing the pattern much enlarged. When the sprites are complete the dot positions are automatically changed into numbers and held in the computer, so making arithmetic unnecessary.

Other graphics utilities are available help produce geometric shapes, rotating shapes and other animated graphics.

Graphics tablets
Some graphics aids allow you to produce impressive designs, even if you have no knowledge of programming at all. One such device is the graphics tablet. This enables you to store pictures in the computer, simply by drawing or tracing them. One type of graphics tablet has a arm with a stylus at the end. Electronic circuits inside the arm form an electrical signal which tells the computer exactly where the stylus is. When the stylus is traced over a drawing, more signals are formed corresponding to points along the path of the stylus. Using all these signals the computer reproduces the path of the stylus as a line on the screen. So a copy the drawing appears as it is traced.

When the drawing has been traced, it easy to alter or colour. The finished picture can be stored on tape or disk for future use.

Another type of graphics tablet has a small coil of wire for tracing the drawing The coil acts as an electromagnet. Wire under the surface of the tablet detect the magnetism, and circuits form the signals that tell the computer where the coil is.

Graphics tablets are also called digitizing tablets or *digitizers* because the signals sent to the computer are in digital form. In other words, they consist of patterns of electricity that represent groups of binary digits (1s and 0s, page 10).

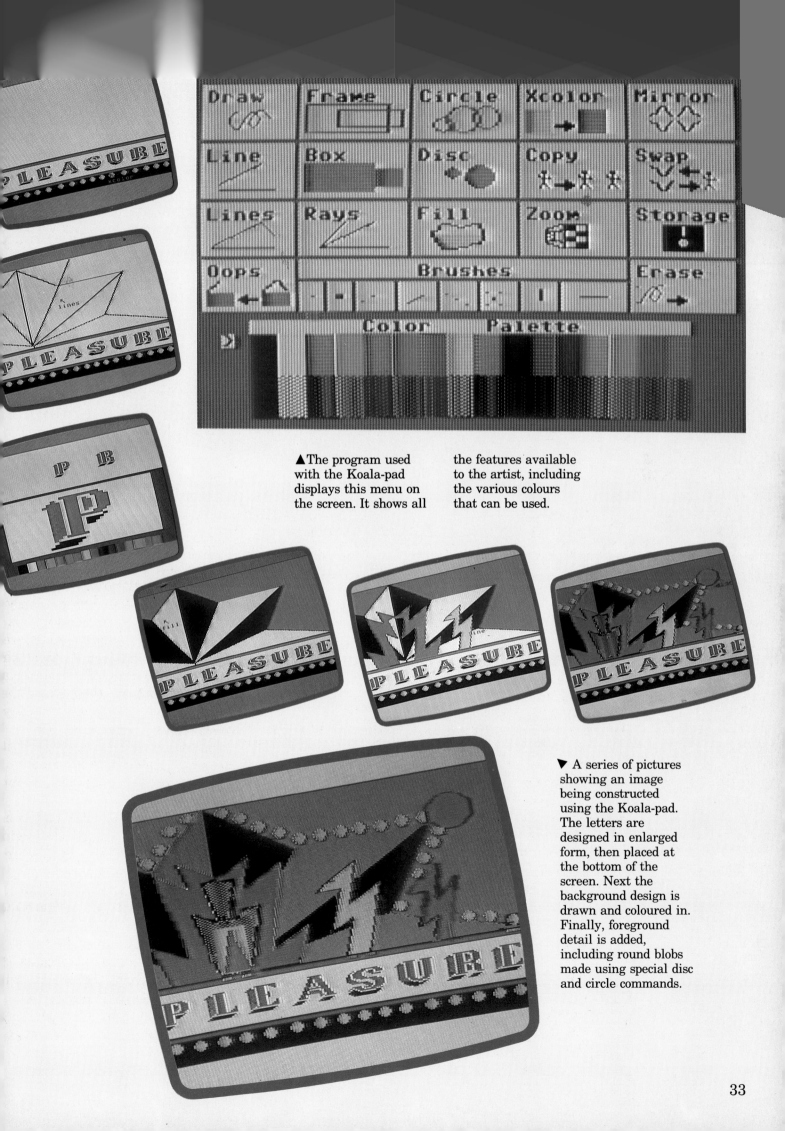

▲ The program used with the Koala-pad displays this menu on the screen. It shows all the features available to the artist, including the various colours that can be used.

▼ A series of pictures showing an image being constructed using the Koala-pad. The letters are designed in enlarged form, then placed at the bottom of the screen. Next the background design is drawn and coloured in. Finally, foreground detail is added, including round blobs made using special disc and circle commands.

►The Digigraph is a graphics aid for storing pictures in a computer. An existing drawing is put on the board and traced with the stylus. Movements of the stylus are automatically changed into electrical signals and fed to the computer. There, the signals are used to form a copy of the drawing on the screen. The screen image can be stored on tape or disk for future use.

▼The Penman Plotter is a computer-controlled robot that can make detailed colour drawings.

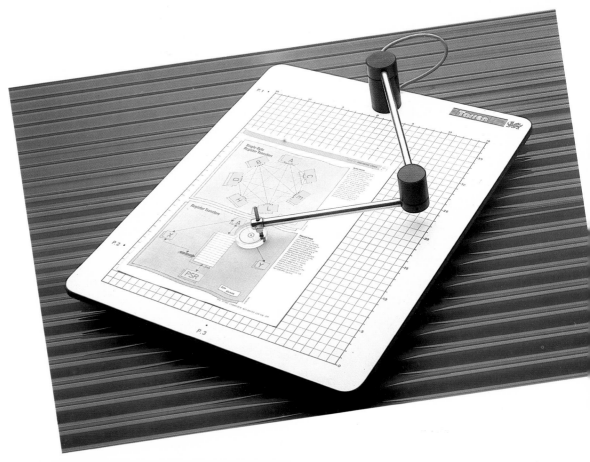

Light pens

With a *light pen*, you can, in effect, dra
directly on the computer screen. What
actually happens is that light from the
faint lines on the screen is first picked
by the pen and changed into an electri
signal. These lines appear to be
permanent, but are being repeatedly
formed in quick succession. From the
timing of the signal formed in the ligh
pen, circuits work out which part of the
screen the pen is on. Then they send a
signal to the computer to make that sa
part of the screen become brighter. Thi
all happens so quickly that the pen
appears to draw a line as it is moved o
the screen.

The electronic paintbox

More detailed designs can be formed or
the screen using a graphics program th
turns the computer into an electronic
paintbox. A 'palette' of colours appears
one part of the screen as a series of col
patches. When a small arrow on the
screen has been moved onto one of the
patches, it acts as if it is a brush that h
been loaded with paint. For it can then
moved over the screen to 'paint' a pictu

The 'brush' may be moved around th
screen using a joystick, *tracker ball*,

◄Among the many impressive features of the Commodore Amiga computer are its highly detailed graphics.

se, or some other controlling device. thickness of the lines formed can be ed. So, in effect, a fine brush can be l for detailed work, and a thick one illing in large areas. Besides loading electronic brush with various colours a the palette, previously stored images be applied too. For example, using an ge of a daisy, a whole field of flowers d be painted on the screen in just nds.

phics on paper

etimes, graphics produced in the puter are required on paper instead of screen. Simple diagrams, formed n block graphics characters, can be oduced on a dot matrix printer. This ne of the great advantages of such a hine – its needles can be made to t various patterns of dots within the a allocated to one printed character. e dot matrix printers can also be le to print user-defined characters, n if these are not available on the puter. So it is sometimes possible to in images on the paper that cannot be ned on the screen.

omplex coloured drawings can be oduced using a *plotter*. The most mon type has a flat support for the

paper. A pen in a motor-driven holder moves over the paper to draw and colour the image according to control signals sent from the computer. Pens of various colours can be fitted, so multicoloured pictures can be produced.

Another type of plotter is a mobile robot that draws a line as it moves about over the paper. This type has the advantage that it can move over a large area and, therefore, can make huge drawings.

▼A flat-bed plotter reproduces a drawing stored in a computer. Each colour is plotted with a different pen.

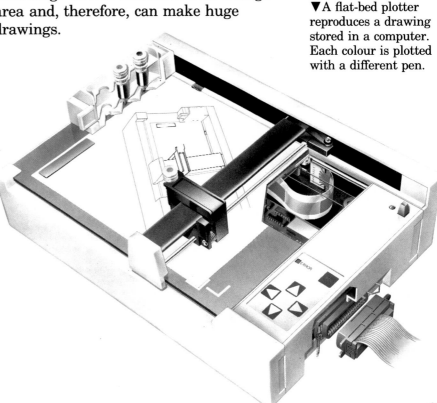

A music making system consisting of a Commodore 64 home computer with a Six-Trak synthesizer and a plug-in unit for storing up to 4000 notes. The screen shows various features that can be selected while composing music.

Pop records are changing, and not just in the style of music that is played. Many of the sounds on today's records are not made by the instruments that you would expect. And sometimes the notes are so unusual that it is hard to imagine what kind of instrument could make such a sound. The cause of this revolution in music is electronics – or, to be more precise, electronic computers, *synthesizers* and sequencers. In a modern sound recording studio one musician with electronic music equipment can make all the sounds of a large orchestra, although he or she may know how to play only one instrument. Besides imitating ordinary instruments, the electronic equipment allows the musician to experiment with sounds, changing them in various ways until a suitable effect is obtained.

Most home computers can make some kind of sound too. With a suitable program a computer with good sound facilities becomes a versatile machine for writing and playing music.

Studio sounds

A synthesizer is an electronic device w circuits that form sound signals. The b synthesizers work with *digital signals*, which consist of patterns of electricity. This makes it easy for circuits like tho in computers to store, alter and combir the signals in various ways. The digita synthesizer is, therefore, like a comput designed solely for working with sound Although the digital signals are easy t handle, they would not sound like note played through a loudspeaker. So, whenever the notes need to be heard, t must be changed into *analogue signals* These resemble ordinary sound waves give rise to musical sounds in the loudspeaker. In the synthesizer, circuit called sound generators change the dig signals into analogue form.

Ordinary, general-purpose computer can be programmed as synthesizers. Bu expensive purpose-built synthesizers, s as the Fairlight and Synclavier, offer a much wider range of facilities.

typical synthesizer has a piano-style
board. When the musician plays notes
he keyboard, they are reproduced on a
speaker. Controls on the synthesizer
w the sound quality to be changed in
ous ways. So the keyboard player can
ate other kinds of instruments, such
rumpets, violins, or drums, or create
rely new kinds of sounds.

metimes the original notes are played
n electric guitar connected to the
thesizer. This gives the musician more
rol. For example, one note can be
ually changed to another by sliding a
er up the guitar string as it vibrates.

npling and sequencers

ead of generating sounds in the
thesizer, real sounds picked up by a
rophone can be changed into digital
als by a process called sampling. The
als are then controlled in the same
as for notes played on the synthesizer
board. A device called a sequencer
ws sequences of sounds to be stored
replayed as required. The sequencer
be a separate unit, but is usually
t into the synthesizer. A useful
ure is that the speed of the music can
aried without altering its pitch – how
h or low the notes sound.

omplete synthesized works are built
n stages, adding a new sound each
e. Typically, the drums are dealt with
t, so that their beat makes it easy to
other parts in time. A computer
trols the whole operation, which is
ed music processing.

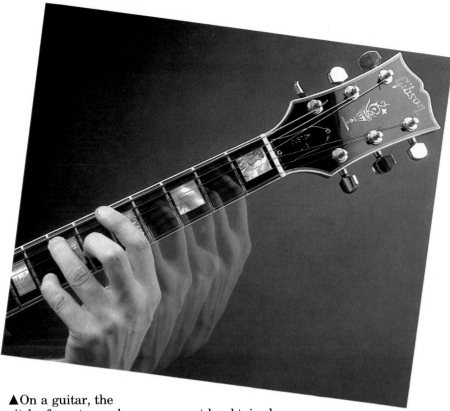

▲On a guitar, the pitch of a note can be changed smoothly by sliding a finger along the string just after plucking it. This effect cannot be obtained on a keyboard, so guitar strings are sometimes used to control synthesizers.

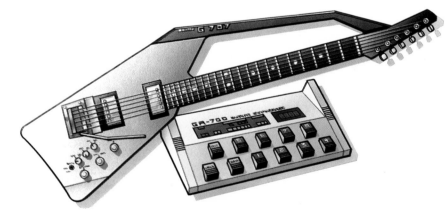

e music program
here shows the
s on the screen in
form of sheet
ic.

▲The Roland GR700 synthesizer uses sounds made on a special guitar.

▼The Synth-Axe is a synthesizer with two sets of strings and a small keyboard. When pressed, the longer strings make contact with the metal frets below. The electrical connections made in this way are used to control the way notes slide from one pitch to another.

e Sound Engineer
ram displays the
rols of a music
hesizer on the
en. Once you have
posed a tune, you
hear what it
ds like on various
ruments.

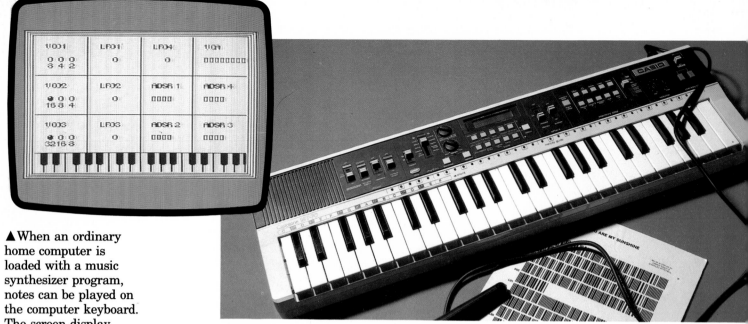

▲When an ordinary home computer is loaded with a music synthesizer program, notes can be played on the computer keyboard. The screen display shows where the notes appear on a piano keyboard.

▼A computer-controlled synthesizer for home music making. Besides storing notes played on the keyboard, this model has a light pen for reading sheet music with the notes specially written in the form of bar code.

Home micro music

Home computers vary greatly in their ability to make sounds. Some can make only simple bleeps, while others can produce an impressive range of sounds, several at a time. Besides music, explosions and other effects may be available to add realism when playing games. The computer may contain a small loudspeaker. But the best sound quality is obtained by connecting the computer to a hi-fi system.

As with graphics, you can learn to program a computer for sound. But it is much easier to use a utility program to help you. The Commodore 64 computer is well-equipped for sound production, and various music utility programs are available for it. One of the best is called the Advanced Music System, produced Firebird Software.

The Advanced Music System allows to write music by pressing keys on the computer keyboard. The notes are displayed like printed music on the screen. At any time, the notes can be played, and their length and quality altered. Once the melody has been completed, other notes can be added to harmonize. The music is stored as code the computer, and an indicator on the screen shows how much of the memory free for storing more music. Short secti of music can be stored and later linked others in order to build up a complete tune.

Once completed, the music can be stored on tape or disk for playing at a later date. And, by adding a printer, a tune can be printed out as sheet music and words added if required.

◄Like other home computers, the Yamaha CX5M can be used for playing games, word processing and many other tasks. But it is designed mainly for the music enthusiast, and comes complete with a plug-in piano-style keyboard.

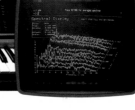

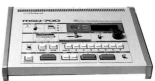

▲Like early electronic computers, the first synthesizers were programmed by making numerous connections. This picture shows Keith Emerson, of the group Emerson Lake and Palmer, using a synthesizer of the 1960s.

...any pop groups use ...Fairlight ...hesizer because it ...versatile.

◄The Synclavier synthesizer has a disk system that can store many complete musical works.

▲The Roland MSQ-700 is a sequencer. It can store and play sequences of up to 6,500 notes.

◄Emu's Drumulator imitates a wide range of drum sounds. Standard rhythms, such as Latin American, are stored on ROM chips.

▼Yamaha's KX5 unit provides synthesizer facilities for the company's CX5 home computer.

39

4 COMMUNICATING WITH COMPUTERS

TALKING COMPUTERS

Like musical sounds, the human voice can be synthesized by a computer. Many micros can now be made to speak, and special-purpose talking computers are being used in many gadgets. One of the first of such devices to find its way into the home was the Speak 'n' Spell educational toy, made by Texas Instruments. A voice asks you to spell a word, and you answer by typing it on a keyboard. The machine then congratulates you if your answer is right, or asks you to try again if it is wrong.

Some electronic clocks now speak the time, although few people really need this feature. But speech synthesizers in vehicles can improve safety. In some cars a voice automatically warns the driver if the seat belt is not fastened, or if the fuel tank is nearly empty.

Besides providing sound effects, some games programs can now make a home

▲My Talking Computer is an educational toy for children aged three and upwards. It is operated by means of a touch-sensitive pad. A coloured overlay is placed over the pad select the program required. Several programs are stored a chip inside the computer.

computer call out the score and give spoken advice. Another kind of program enables the computer to speak words th you type on the keyboard. So you can make the computer say anything you choose.

Computers can also be made to understand words spoken into a microphone. This enables you to answe questions and enter information into th computer just by speaking, instead of b typing on the keyboard.

w computers have a built-in speech
hesizer. Others require an extra chip
e plugged in, or an additional unit to
onnected for this purpose. Speech is
ed in computers in the same way as
ic. The sounds are changed into
tal electrical signals, which the
puter can store just like any other
rmation. It is much simpler and
per to record speech on a tape
rder. The reason for holding speech in
mputer is that words, phrases or
ences can be produced according to
mands in a program. The program
rmines which words are to be spoken,
obtains the speech signals from the
nory where they are stored. These
tal signals are then changed into
logue signals – the form that produces
appropriate sounds when passed
ugh a loudspeaker.

gments of sound

kind of speech synthesizer contains a
e of sound fragments called phonemes.
se are used as building blocks for
ing words. For example, the word
k' would be formed from three
nemes: b-oo-k. The required phonemes
be selected in various ways.

ome systems will speak words typed in
n English. The main problem here is
parts of words with similar spelling
need to be pronounced differently.
example, in 'thought' and 'though',
'ough' part sounds quite different.
, some words with identical spelling
pronounced differently, as in the
tence: 'This road may lead to the lead
e'. To ensure correct pronunciation of
words, the synthesizer system needs to
erstand a great deal about English, or
tever language is being used. The
(and most expensive) systems work
l, but the cheapest synthesizers that
pt plain English often get the
nunciation wrong. This can be
rcome by changing the spelling of any
ds that are mispronounced. For
mple, if 'cattle' comes out sounding
e like 'cat-lee', you might try spelling
word as 'catel' instead. This is no
at problem if your aim is simply to

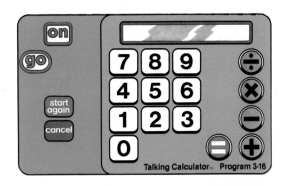

**My Talking
Computer in Action**

◀Talking Story:
The computer speaks
each word as it is
pressed by the child.

◀Sentence Maker:
When the child presses
the question mark, the
computer speaks a
word. The child then
tries to press the right
word key.

◀Talking Calculator:
This works like an
ordinary calculator,
except that it speaks
the figures as they are
entered and then
announces the answer.

◀Telling the Time:
The clock is fitted
above the touch pad.
The computer tells
what time is indicated
when the child sets the
hands.

make the computer speak a certain
message. But, if you want the computer to
read various pieces of text, frequent
mistakes are annoying, and can make
some sentences impossible to understand.

Other systems do not attempt to
convert ordinary words into speech.
Instead, you have to spell each word in a
special way that tells the computer which
phonemes to use.

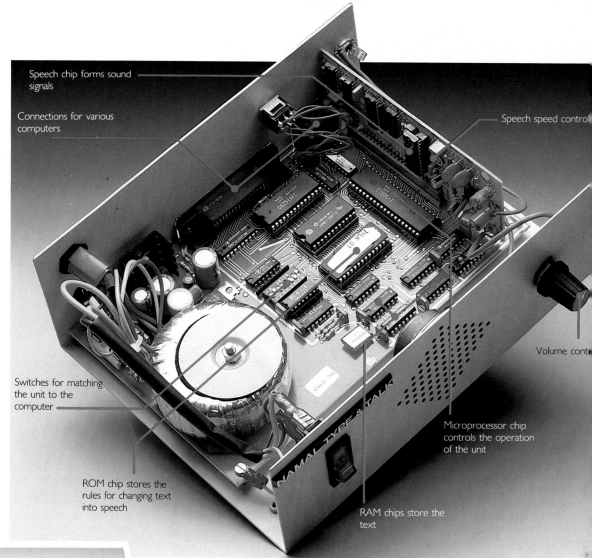

Speech chip forms sound signals

Connections for various computers

Speech speed control

Switches for matching the unit to the computer

Volume control

Microprocessor chip controls the operation of the unit

ROM chip stores the rules for changing text into speech

RAM chips store the text

▲In science fiction, robots like Robby from the film *Forbidden Planet*, can talk with humans. Today, some real robots can understand simple, spoken commands, and also talk to their users.

NAMAL TYPE & TALK

▲The Namal Type & Talk unit is a speech synthesizer designed for use with a home micro. The synthesizer speaks words that are typed on the computer keyboard.

▶Two simple speech synthesizers for home computers: the Cheetah Sweetalker (**left**) for the Sinclair Spectrum, and the Currah Speech 64 for the Commodore 64 computer.

Word stores

For some computers, you can buy a speech chip to plug into a spare socket inside. The chip is a form of ROM (Read Only Memory). It contains a permanent record of many common words. These words were originally spoken into a microphone, and the signals from it changed into digital form. Sentences can be made up by selecting suitable words from the chip. This is done using simple commands in a program. The words are then reproduced through a loudspeaker. The sound quality is usually very good, and you may even recognize the voice of the person who originally spoke the words.

Instead of using someone else's words, you can record your own using additional equipment connected to the computer. A few of the more expensive micros have this facility built in. The words are held in code in the computer's RAM (Random Access Memory), and can be stored on tape or disk for future use.

EECH RECOGNITION

make a computer understand what
say, a speech recognition unit must
connected to it. You talk into a
rophone plugged into this unit. First,
have to give the system some samples
he words that you want it to recognize.
you speak the words and they are
ed in digital form. Then the unit can
pare anything you say with the words
as stored. A program in the computer
kes it carry out some action when a
d is recognized. For example, you
ld make an object move around the
screen simply by using spoken commands
such as UP, DOWN, RIGHT, LEFT and
STOP.

With a computer able to both talk and
understand speech, you could hold a
conversation with it in English, or in
some other language. However, until
cheap speech recognition units become
faster to respond, and more reliable in
operation, the keyboard will continue to
be the main means of getting information
into the computer.

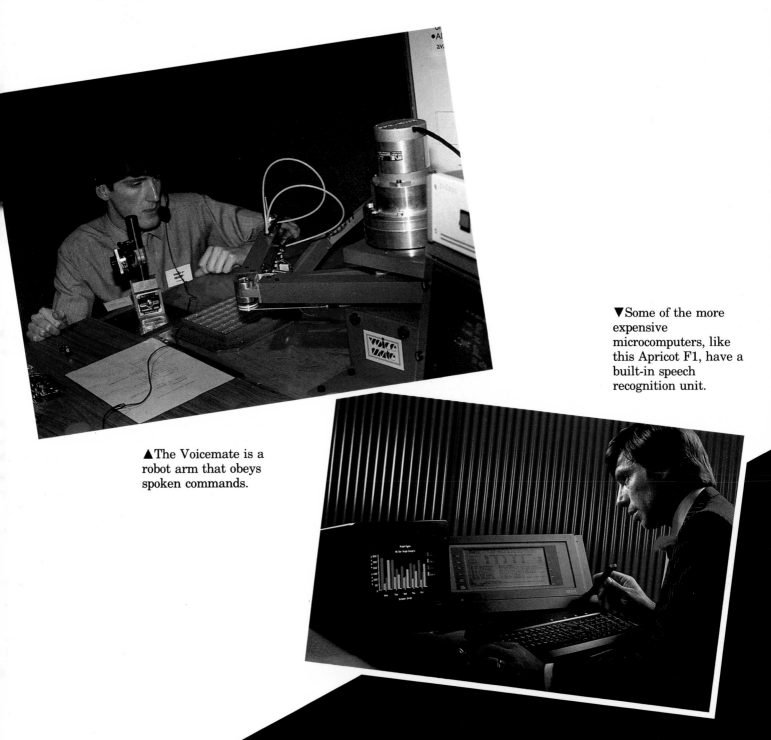

▼Some of the more
expensive
microcomputers, like
this Apricot F1, have a
built-in speech
recognition unit.

▲The Voicemate is a
robot arm that obeys
spoken commands.

43

COMMUNICATING BY COMPUTER

Like the telephone, the computer allows people to communicate. Computerized information appears on our television screens in the form of videotext. And we may find a computer talking to us when we make a telephone call. We can also use a computer to exchange messages and information with other computers, which might be in the same building, but could be thousands of kilometres away.

Of course, it is often easier to exchange information by talking to people. But transferring text by computer avoids the errors that can occur when someone tries to write down everything you say on the telephone. Another advantage is that information can be transferred to a person's computer at any time and left there for them to look at whenever they wish. This is particularly useful for communicating between countries on opposite sides of the world, as daytime at one end of the line is night-time at the other end.

Computers on the line

Some telephone answering machines now use a computerized speech synthesizer to talk to callers. As a synthesizer has no moving parts, machines like this are more reliable than those that replay a messa[ge] recorded on tape. When such a machin[e] connected to a number that you call, th[e] message in the synthesizer is simply replayed down the line, but the machin[e] still records messages from callers on a[n] ordinary tape recorder. This is because [a] great deal of computer memory would [be] needed to store long messages.

Some large companies have a system for storing telephone messages in a powerful computer called a message centre. Suppose that you try to phone a[ ]friend who works at the company, but [he] or she is not in when you make the cal[l.] The switchboard operator takes your message and types it on a computer keyboard. The message is then stored i[n] the computer as text. On returning to [the] building, your friend can read your message on a computer screen.

He or she can also receive your mess[age] without returning to the building. For [the] computer can use the stored text to synthesize speech. So your friend can simply telephone the company and get [a] computer to read out any messages tha[t] have been left. This kind of system is known as voicemail.

►Computer communications now play an important part in businesses where up-to-date information is needed. In this bank, any changes in foreign currency exchange rates are immediately flashed onto the computer screen on the wall.

...t by telephone

...h a computer and suitable equipment
...onnect it to a telephone line, you can
...in messages and information from
...er computers in the form of text. You
... just want to read what comes up on
...screen, but you could store the text on
...e or disk, or get it printed – just as if
...words had been typed on your own
...puter. This kind of communication
...many uses.

...order to send and receive computer
...als by means of the telephone line,
...must connect a device called a *modem*
...ween your computer and the telephone
...e. The modem changes the signals from
...r computer into a form that can pass
...ugh the telephone system. It also
...nges incoming signals into the form
...t your computer can understand. In
...se two processes, the signals are
...nged using techniques called
...dulation and DEModulation, hence
...name 'modem'.

...ome modems are plugged directly into
...telephone socket. Another type sends
...receives its signals as sounds passed
...ugh the telephone handset. A modem
...this is called an *acoustic coupler*.

...siness communications

...increasing number of people work at
...e instead of going to an office each
...They use a computer to communicate
...h the company that they work for.
...rmation that they need is left on the
...pany's computer and can be
...sferred to their own computer via the
...phone system. The company's
...puter will also store any information
...t to it by the person working at home.
...alespeople travelling around the
...ntry can communicate with their
...pany office using a portable computer
...end and receive information through a
...lic telephone. Details of orders
...ained during the day can be sent to
...company in the evening. The next
..., the company can look at the orders
...get the goods ready for despatch.

...vate communications

...yone with suitable computer

equipment and a telephone can
communicate with other computers. Some
enthusiasts run free services called
Bulletin Board Systems (BBS). Their
telephone numbers are published in
computer magazines. When you telephone
a BBS, the computer there will allow you
to leave messages. You could, for
example, ask for help with a computing
problem. The next time you contact the

▶Many viewdata
advertisements include
illustrations, but the
graphics are of poor
quality on most
systems. Better
graphics could be
transmitted, but the
more detail included,
the longer it takes to
send all the
information through
the telephone system.
Having a low-quality
system avoids
excessive delays
between selecting a
service and receiving
the picture.

◀With a portable
computer and modem,
you can contact other
computers from a
public telephone box.

system you may find that someone has left a helpful message for you. Most computer enthusiasts are only too willing to share their knowledge.

Many other services are available if you pay a fee to join. An enormous amount of information on almost any subject can be obtained in this way. You may have to make an additional payment each time you use the service, but some information is usually provided at no extra charge. The computerized store of information is called a database.

▼Home computer equipment set up to receive viewdata services. The computer is linked to the telephone by means of a modem with an acoustic coupler.

►The prism modem is wired directly to the telephone line to give extremely reliable communications with viewdata services.

DATABASES

Databases are designed to make it easy for anyone to find the information that they want. An index system shows you the subjects covered by the system and you make your selection by typing in on the keyboard the appropriate word or number for the information you want. The computer then obtains the information from a magnetic disk.

▲ Obtaining holiday travel information at home by means of a viewdata service. Here, a special handset is used to select the required information, which comes via the telephone line and is displayed on an ordinary television set. The set can also receive teletext information, which is broadcast along with television programmes.

ravel agents use vdata services to in information ut seats on aircraft to book tickets for r customers.

◄ American Express provide this viewdata service giving aircraft arrival and departure information. Any of the information listed can be obtained on the screen by typing the key number on the computer.

With a suitable program, any home computer can be used to set up a database system for personal use. But the professional systems that can be contacted by telephone are many times more powerful.

One of the best-known computer information services is a US system set up in 1979 and called The Source.

Through this system, subscribers have access to information from about 1000 databases. Besides specialized informat on a wide range of subjects, The Source provides much of general interest. For example, you can find out what is on television. And, if you forget to watch a episode of your favourite TV series, The Source will tell you what you missed.

►Most viewdata systems use simple graphics. These can be transmitted quickly, but cannot reproduce fine detail, and curved lines look distinctly jagged. The Mupid system shown here is a high quality viewdata system. Although the graphics are excellent, each highly detailed picture takes about two minutes to be transmitted by means of the telephone line. This is why the system has attracted little interest in most countries. However, a high quality viewdata system has been adopted in Canada.

COMMUNICATING FOR FUN

Some services also store computer games for subscribers to play. You either transfer the program into your own computer and play it on that, or the program may remain in the main computer, your own computer being used just to control the action. Because the main computer has a large memory, it can store elaborate programs that are much too long to fit into the average home micro. So you can enjoy games with

features that are normally impossible t produce.

In an ordinary adventure game you often meet imaginary people or creatur on your travels. But, when connected b the telephone line to an adventure gam running on a powerful computer, you m also meet other people who are playing the game. Imagine that you are trying find a wizard who can give you the magical powers you will need in order t

rcome some danger. You enter a room
a message on the screen tells you
someone is there. You type in the
stion: 'Are you the wizard?', but find
you have met another player when
get the reply: 'No! My name's Eric.
looking for the wizard too, but I've
n stuck here for hours. Any idea how
get out?'

ou may then spend some time
ussing with the other player the
tes you have followed so far. And you
may exchange information on how to
overcome various problems that occur. Or
you may forget about the game and talk
about other things with your fellow
adventurer.

The one great problem with games like
this is that you can easily find you have
been using the phone line for an hour or
more. This can make you unpopular with
others in your home who want to use the
phone, and the next phone bill may be an
unpleasant surprise.

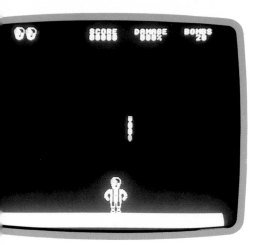

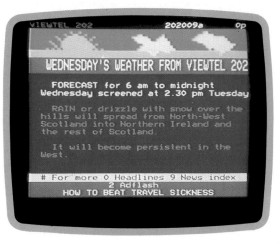

◄Six screen displays
from the Micronet
viewdata service for
computer enthusiasts.

HELPING THE HANDICAPPED

▶Although this girl cannot speak or control her limbs, she is able to control the computer using a device on her head. It is called a photonic wand. Here she is pointing the wand at the screen to play a game (**right**) and to draw a pattern (**far right**).

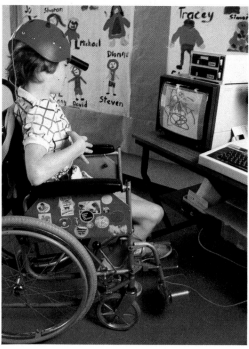

Microcomputers now help handicapped people to do things that were once impossible, especially in the field of communications. Deaf people can now use the telephone, and so can people who are unable to speak. The blind can read ordinary books and typed letters. And even those unable to move their limbs can use computers.

Aids for the deaf and mute

People who are deaf, or who cannot speak can use standard computer equipment to communicate by telephone. With a modem to link their computer to the telephone line, they can exchange messages with others who have similar equipment. Words typed on the keyboard at one end of the line can be read from the screen at the other end. Handicapped people with this equipment can also make use of the many computerized information services available (page 46).

The main problem for such people is that many of their friends do not have the right equipment for this kind of communication. However, a speech synthesizer will enable a person who cannot speak to communicate with anyone by telephone. It can change words typed on the keyboard into speech, which can then be sent along the telephone line. Because typing can be slow, it helps if the

main message is typed before making t call. Then it can be played down the li when contact has been made.

A deaf person wanting to understand speech received by telephone needs a speech recognition unit capable of changing the speech into words on the screen. Unfortunately, units that can accurately recognize whole sentences spoken at speed and with various accen are not available. However, in some areas, computer-equipped centres have been set up to help the deaf. People wit a message for a deaf person can read it a computer operator at the centre. The operator types the message on a compu and then sends it via the telephone line the deaf person's computer, where it appears on the screen.

Blind aids

Some blind people now carry out office work with the aid of word processors. A speech synthesizer can be made to announce each letter or numeral as it i typed on the keyboard. So the blind person becomes aware of any mistakes and can correct them immediately. Completed documents can be read back from the word processor by a speech synthesizer. Or the blind person can connect a device called a braille link. T has rows of pins that rise to form braill

...tterns of the words. A trained blind
...rson can quickly read these patterns by
...uch.
...Ordinary typed documents can be read
... means of a device called an Opticon. A
...y television camera is moved across the
...es of print, and its signals are sent to a
...it with a touch pad on top. Pins on the
...d vibrate so that the shape of each
...ter can be felt. The Opticon can also be
...ed for reading words from the screen.

...her aids

...me people are unable to move their
...bs. But they may be able to operate
...e computer keyboard using a bent rod
...ed to their head. Another approach is to
...ect the letters or numbers from a
...ture of a keyboard on the screen. One
...y of selecting the required characters is
... use simple switches to move a marker
...und the screen. The switches are
...ked by moving the head.

...Sometimes it is more convenient for the
...abled person to use a device called a
...otonic wand. This works like a light
...n, but does not have to be in contact
...th the computer screen. The wand,
...ich is fixed to a helmet worn by the
...abled person, is simply pointed at the
...een. Letters displayed on the screen
...n be selected by pointing at them.
...other part of the screen shows the
...rds formed by the selected letters. Like
...ight pen, the wand can also be used for
...awing pictures on the screen, and to
...ntrol the computer when playing
...mes.

...Disabled people with a little more
...ntrol of their arm movements can use a
...ecially designed keyboard with just a
...v large keys.

...ncept keyboards

...me flat keyboards can be covered with
...lastic sheet called an overlay. Pictures
... the overlay are positioned over certain
...ys. This kind of device is called a
...ncept keyboard. A program in the
...nputer makes it respond in the right
...y when any particular picture is
...essed. For example, the overlay might
...ow arrows pointing in various
...ections. Pressing any arrow could move
...marker over the screen to draw a

diagram. A variety of overlays and
programs are available for the concept
keyboard, which has proved especially
useful as an aid to teaching handicapped
children.

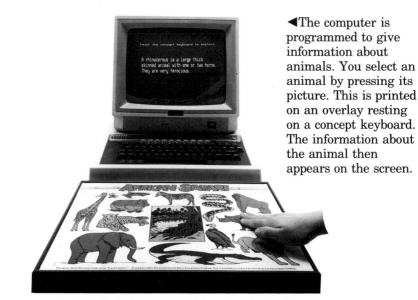

◀The computer is
programmed to give
information about
animals. You select an
animal by pressing its
picture. This is printed
on an overlay resting
on a concept keyboard.
The information about
the animal then
appears on the screen.

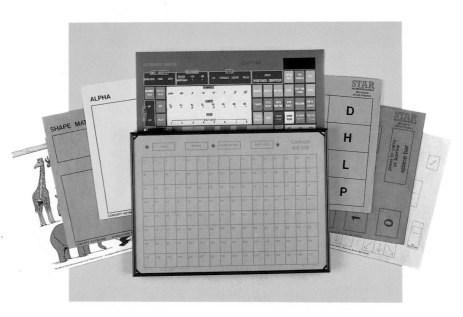

▲A concept keyboard
is a flat pad divided
into squares. Switches
underneath detect
when any square is
pressed. It is used in
place of an ordinary
keyboard. To make it
easier to use by
handicapped people,
groups of squares can
be made to produce the
same effect, whichever
one is pressed. A
printed sheet called an
overlay shows what
each part of the board
does. For example,
large areas of the
board can be pressed to
print a letter or
numeral on the screen.

BEHIND THE COUNTER

For many years, factories and offices have benefited from the use of computers. And now, because prices have fallen so much, almost any firm can afford a computer. In fact, more and more firms are finding that they cannot afford to be without one. Suitable equipment and the necessary specialized programs are available for hotels, restaurants, bars, libraries, supermarkets, lawyers, auctioneers, airlines and many other businesses, services and professions. Even individual shopkeepers are discovering the benefits of having a computer behind the counter

Helping business efficiency

Here's one example of how a computer can help a small business. Early in the morning, vans deliver bundles of newspapers and magazines to newspaper shops. From these, the staff usually make up mixed bundles for delivery to the streets that the shop serves. The staff have to look at the order book to see what needs to be delivered to each house. Then they have to take the right papers and magazines from the bundles, and mark them all with a house number so that the delivery boy or girl knows whose they are.

When a person goes to the shop to pay the bill, an assistant again looks at the order book to see what the weekly bill should be, but has to make a deduction for some reason, one of the papers or magazines was not published that week. All this means a great deal of work, so computer systems have been developed help.

First, full details, including costs, of all papers and magazines to be delivered to each address are entered in the computer. This information is then stored on disk. Each morning, a printer connected to the computer prints a list for each street, showing how many copies of each item are required. The staff then take these papers and magazines from the bundles delivered to the shop to form a bundle for the street. But they do not have to mark the items with house numbers. For the printer also supplies a list for the delivery person, showing what to deliver to each house.

When a paper or magazine is not published, this information is entered in the computer. Then, when a customer comes to pay the bill, the printer produces an up-to-date account, automatically deducting the right amount for missing items.

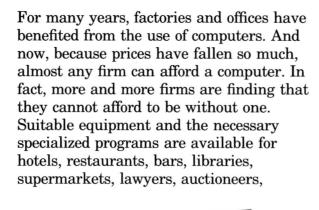

▼For a one-person firm, a home microcomputer may be all that is needed to help the business run more smoothly.

codes for convenience

of the most common places to find
puters at work is in supermarkets.
use a supermarket sells so many
rent products, a lot of work is
lved in knowing the quantity of each
uct in stock at any time. Keeping too
y of an item uses money that could
pent on other things and wastes
able storage space. But the super-
ket must avoid running out of items.
he problem is solved by a computer
em for reading bar codes – the
erns of thick and thin lines printed on
packages of many products. These
es tell a computer what the product is.
here are two ways in which the bar
es can be read at the checkout. In one
hod the item is passed over a slot in
counter. A light shining up through
slot reflects off the bar code. In the
nd method a pen, called a bar code
ler, is run across the bars. The pen
minates the pattern and a sensor in
pen picks up the reflected light. In
systems the reflected light is
nged into electricity. In this way the
code pattern is changed into a pattern
lectrical pulses. These are fed into a
puter which recognizes the product
n the pattern of pulses. The computer
tains a record of all items and their
es, so it knows how much to charge
customer. This amount is
omatically printed on the bill, and a
l produced when all the customer's

items have been read.

Information about the sale is kept in
the computer and used at the end of the
day to decide the items to be re-ordered.

▲This shows how the
number 72 can be
stored in a bar code for
reading by means of
computer equipment.
In the code used here,
patterns of five wide or
narrow bars represent
the numerals. Special
3-bar codes are used to
tell the computer when
to start and stop
reading the coded
numbers.

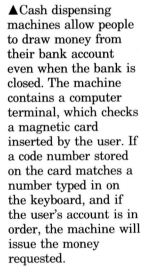

▲Cash dispensing
machines allow people
to draw money from
their bank account
even when the bank is
closed. The machine
contains a computer
terminal, which checks
a magnetic card
inserted by the user. If
a code number stored
on the card matches a
number typed in on
the keyboard, and if
the user's account is in
order, the machine will
issue the money
requested.

◄As the tip of the
reader is moved over
the bar code on the
chocolate wrapper, the
sensor picks up light
reflected from the
spaces between the
bars. It changes the
light into electrical
signals. The digitizer
changes the signals
from the light sensor
into patterns of
electricity that the
computer can
recognize.

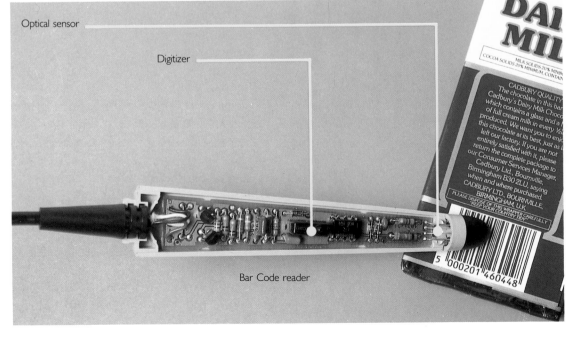

Optical sensor

Digitizer

Bar Code reader

ROBOTS

Since the 1920s, robots have featured in many science fiction stories and films. These robots usually have two arms, and a head that enables them to see and speak. They also move about on legs, and can deal with almost any problem that confronts them. Most real-life robots are quite different. One common type is fixed in position and has a single arm for moving objects around. And robots that move about usually have wheels instead of legs, or 'float' just above the surface of the ground. However, for entertainment, some robots are made to look as much like humans as possible. Robots like this are seen in films, wax-work museums, stores and amusement parks. In each case a computer controls all the robot's movements.

▼Zeaker is a robot with collision sensors at the sides and ends. If it strikes an object, the bumper strip pushes one of the buttons. This sends a signal by cable to a computer, which immediately stops the robot. If required, it will try moving in another direction. Like the turtle, Zeaker is used mainly for teaching.

THE ROBOT ARM

The robot arm is widely used in large manufacturing industries. This is beca it can be used in so many ways. The t performed by this kind of robot can be divided into four groups: moving items from one position to another; assembli parts; holding tools during the manufacturing process; and holding pa during manufacture.

A typical arm is mounted on a fixed base so that it can swivel from side to side and pivot up and down. It may ha a joint like an elbow about half-way a its length, and a sliding wrist section r allow the arm's length to change. Vari grippers, tools and other devices are bolted to the end of the arm to suit the task to be done.

The arm is usually powered by elect motors or by hydraulics. A hydraulic system uses a liquid under pressure to force pistons to move along cylinders. Each piston controls a different arm movement.

►Welding is the m common task given industrial robots. T Lansing robot arm shown here is weld together metal brackets.

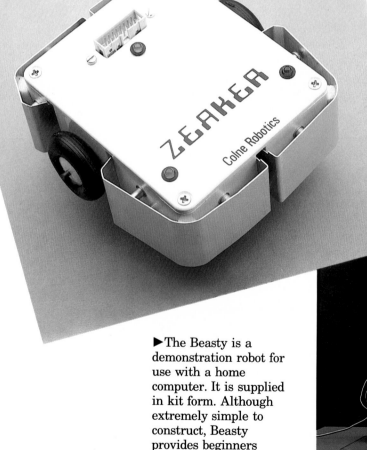

►The Beasty is a demonstration robot for use with a home computer. It is supplied in kit form. Although extremely simple to construct, Beasty provides beginners with valuable experience in robotics.

A musical robot performs for the public at Japan's Tsukuba Expo 85. A synthesizer would be more efficient, but the purpose here is to demonstrate, in an entertaining way, some of the complex actions that can be performed using a robot.

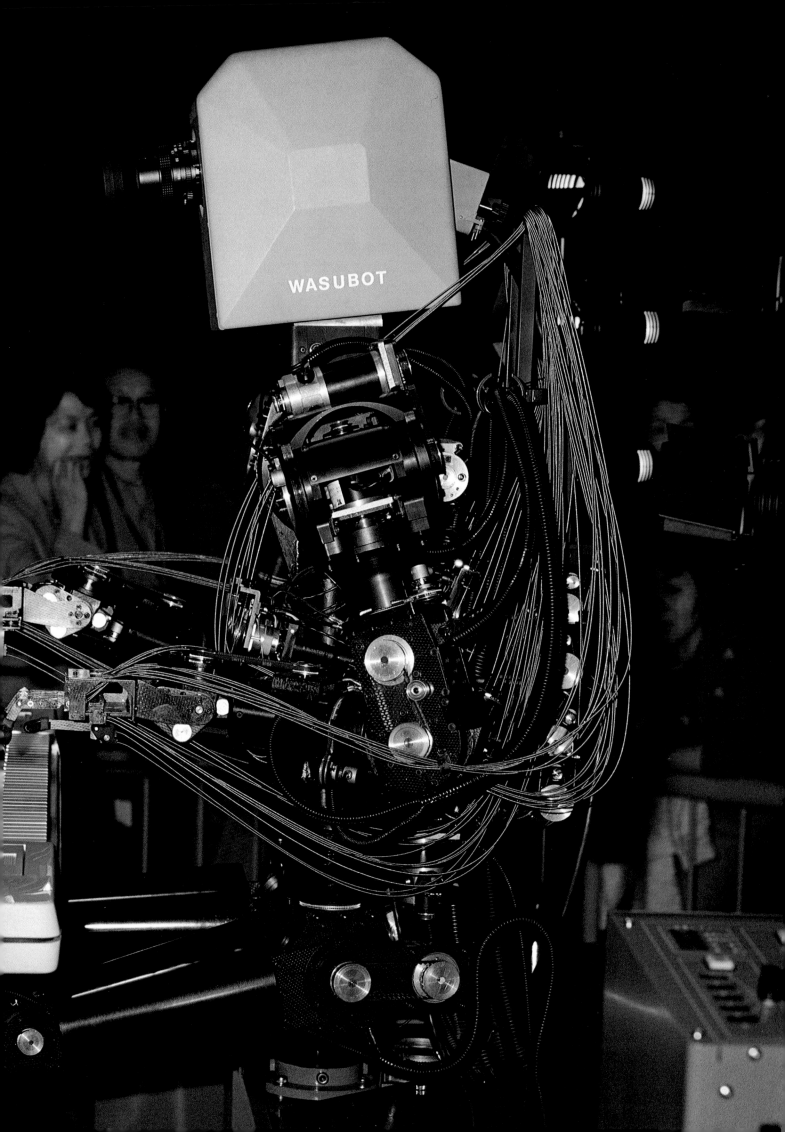

As an exercise in control, this robot arm has been made to place an egg in its cup. If you try this, use something solid instead of an egg until you are sure that all is well. Otherwise, the robot may grip too tightly and crush the egg, or even drop it over the edge of the table.

▼ Sensors on the gripper of a robot arm allow it to carry out delicate operations. The proximity sensor tells a computer when the arm is close enough to the egg to pick it up. The computer then makes the gripper close. The tactile (touch) sensors detect when an object has been gripped and stop the grippers from closing any farther. The strain gauge measures the precise force applied to the egg. A sudden decrease in this force could mean that the eggshell had started to collapse.

Pick and place

Many factories use robot arms to move items from one position to the next during the manufacturing process. Robots are ideally suited to this kind of handling task, which is known as pick and place. Unlike humans, robots can shift heavy

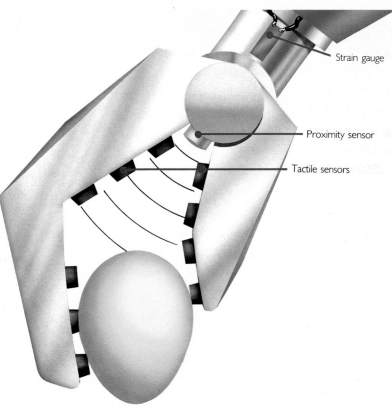

Strain gauge

Proximity sensor

Tactile sensors

items all day long without a break. And they can work faster too. The first robots stopped and started abruptly and so their movements were rather jerky. But modern robots move more smoothly and can position items with great precision.

For handling items, the robot arm is usually equipped with a gripping device. If one of the standard grips is unsuitable for a particular job, a special one can be made. But sometimes a different handling device is used. For example, items with smooth surfaces, which might slip through the robot's grip, can be picked by a suction pad mounted on the end of the arm.

Assembly

The assembly of various parts to form a unit is a more difficult task for a robot. It must select the parts in the right order and hold them in a certain way so that they will fit together. If the parts are in separate piles, then selection is easy. The computer is simply programmed to make the robot pick from the different piles in particular order. But, if the parts are mixed up, the robot will need some way of telling them apart. One way of doing this is to fit a small television camera to the arm. The picture from the camera is fed into the computer, which is programmed to recognize the shapes of all the components. When the arm passes near the next part needed for assembly, the computer recognizes it and makes the arm pick it up.

Many pieces of equipment are assembled by robots. But it is still easier or cheaper, or both, to assemble most items using simple machines or human workers.

Tools for the job

The robot arm is used mainly to weld together metal parts of motor cars. The arm is fitted with an electric welding tool which clamps over the metal to be joined. A burst of electricity then passes through the tool and metal, making a small part of the metal melt and join together.

With suitable tools fixed to the arm, a robot can carry out other tasks, such as paint spraying and applying adhesives. The computer is often programmed for

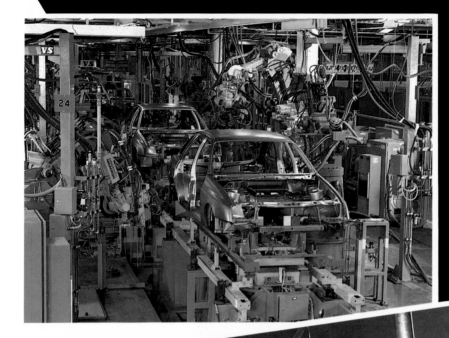

▶A cluster of robot tools in action on a Ford Sierra assembly line.

▶Robot arms are useful for doing dirty work in unpleasant conditions. Here a small arm is cleaning pieces of hot metal, just after they have been cast into shape. A human would have to wait for them to cool down, but the robot is not affected by the heat.

se jobs by copying a skilled human ng the job. The worker first moves the and tool through all the necessary tions. The arm detects every movement de and feeds the information to the puter as electrical signals. The signals stored in the computer and used to trol the robot arm when it carries out job. So the robot immediately acquires expert's skill in that particular task.

lding parts
ome processes, the tools or nufacturing equipment are fixed in

position, and the materials undergoing treatment are moved. For example, a sheet of metal may be placed in a heavy machine that presses a pattern into it. A robot arm is usually very efficient at handling materials in such cases. Also, it can work in conditions that humans find unpleasant, dangerous, or even impossible. Many manufacturing processes involve heating things to high temperatures, or using chemicals that give off dangerous fumes. With robots handling the materials, people can keep out of harm's way.

ROBOTS ON THE MOVE

►The floor turtle is a mobile robot used in the classroom. It teaches children about angles, distances and shapes. At the same time, it shows how computers can control robots.

In some modern factories, robots glide along the floor, transporting parts or finished goods. At the headquarters of the Westinghouse Corporation in Grand Rapids, Michigan, a small robot trundles around delivering mail to employees. And a larger robot vehicle called a People Mover takes visitors on a guided tour of the building.

Mobile robots can also work in areas where a human could be in danger. Some security forces use robots to investigate devices that could be bombs. As the robot approaches a suspect object, it sends back television pictures of it to the security personnel, who are some distance away.

Many mobile robots are equipped with an arm, which enables them to handle dangerous items, such as radioactive materials used for atomic research.

Turtles in the classroom
In the classroom, miniature robots are used to teach the principles of computing and robotics. One such device is the *turtle*, which moves about the floor, changing direction according to commands sent from the computer. The path taken can be marked on a large sheet of paper by a pen attached to the turtle.

Talkative robots
The most entertaining robots are modern versions of the kind that have been appearing in science fiction films for years. But, instead of having bodies and limbs that are obviously made from metal, they closely resemble humans. And they can often speak with a human voice

too. Robots like this sometimes inform visitors about the various attractions in stores and tourist areas. You could, for example, find Buffalo Bill telling you about the history of the Wild West.

Sensors and control
Mobile robots that move over a small area are often connected to a fixed computer means of a cable. But such a connection unsuitable for robots that wander farther afield, or that move in places where the cable could get caught or tangled.

The Westinghouse People Mover carries its own computer on board. Wires under the factory floor carry electrical signals that the vehicle picks up and feeds into its computer. These signals are used to guide the vehicle in its tour around the building.

The device that picks up the signals from the underfloor wires is called a sensor. Various kinds of sensors enable robots to travel around without bumping into people or objects.

Some robots can follow a white line painted on the floor. To do this, the robot shines a light on the floor and picks up the reflected light with one or more light sensors. The white paint reflects a high proportion of light and the sensors turn this into strong electrical signals. If the robot strays off the line, the signal strength falls. This change is detected by the computer, which then sends signals the robot to steer it back on course.

Other robots find their way by means ultrasonics – sound waves that are too high to be heard by the human ear. The robot emits the waves and picks up the reflections from nearby objects. The length of the split-second delay between sending and receiving the signals tells the computer how far an object is from the robot. If its path is blocked, the robot will stop to avoid a collision. It will then wait until the path is clear, or may be programmed to seek an alternative route.

From all this, it may seem that some robots are extremely intelligent. Certain robots can perform some tasks much better than we can. But it will be a very long time before they can even begin to challenge the intelligence and wide-ranging abilities of human beings.

▼This close-up picture shows the interior of a typical turtle. Note the two electric motors that allow the drive wheels to be controlled independently for maximum mobility.

▼The Valiant turtle appeals to younger children as it is made to resemble the animal for which it is named. Unlike most turtles, it has its own battery, and so draws no power from the computer.

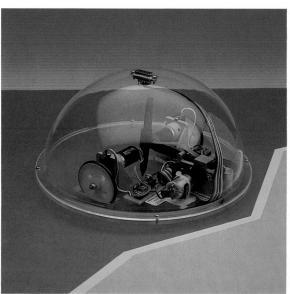

◄Two cheap, robot-like toys from the Movits range. Although they are designed to work on their own, some enthusiasts have found ways of controlling them by means of computers.

►Hero-1 is a mobile robot with an arm. It is battery powered and has a built-in computer, thus making it completely self-contained. Hero can talk, and some people keep one in the home as kind of pet.

GLOSSARY

Acoustic coupler A type of modem, with a pair of rubber cups that grip the mouthpiece and earpiece of a telephone handset. The coupler enables computer signals to be sent and received acoustically (as sounds) through the handset.

Analogue signal An electrical signal that varies in an analogous (similar) way to a sound wave, temperature variation, or some other continuously changing quantity. Analogue signals must be converted into digital form so that they can be used in a computer.

BASIC An easy-to-use language for giving instructions to a computer. BASIC is an abbreviation for Beginners' All-purpose Symbolic Instruction Code. It is the programming language used in almost every home computer.

Binary system A system for counting in twos. In our everyday decimal system, we count in tens, using the digits 0 to 9. In binary, the only digits used are 0 and 1. Binary numbers may be much longer than their decimal equivalents, but they are easier to store in computers. For example, the numbers 128 and 129 appear in binary as 10000000 and 10000001.

Bit One of the two digits, 0 and 1, used in the binary system. Bit is short for binary digit.

Bug A fault in a computer or in a computer program. It is extremely difficult to be absolutely sure that all bugs have been eliminated, because it is almost impossible to write a program that can cope with all circumstances and possibilities when used by perhaps many thousands of people.

Byte A group of bits that represents a binary number and can be stored in a computer. Originally the word byte was short for 'by eight', and meant a group of 8 bits. But the word is now used to refer to larger groups of bits, too. The size of a computer's memory is expressed as the number of bytes that it can store. In most microcomputers each byte consists of 8 16 bits.

Chip A small slice of silicon crystal on which tiny electronic components have been assembled to form a circuit. The chip, or integrated circuit, has a protective plastic or ceramic exterior.

Command An instruction given to the computer from the keyboard or by a program. For example, in BASIC, the command LIST will cause the program the computer to be listed on the screen.

Cursor A marker on the screen that shows where the next character will appear. The cursor usually consists of a square or horizontal line, and may flash on and off to make its position obvious.

Daisy wheel A device used in high-quality printers. Type characters on thi flexible strips are fixed to a central disc

Database A store of information (data held in a computer system. The informa is usually stored on a magnetic disk. A program enables any information required to be found quickly and displa on the screen or printed on paper.

Digital signal In a computer, binary numbers are stored and handled as dig signals. For example, the number 10011011 can be stored in one 8-bit b of memory. A small fixed voltage can represent each 1, and the absence of a voltage can represent each 0. Digital signals are used in computers because they are easy to store, and simple electronic circuits can reliably determin whether each bit is a 1 or a 0.

Digitizer A device for getting pictures into a computer. A picture is drawn or traced, and the digitizer sends digital signals to the computer to make the sa picture appear on the screen.

Disk The magnetic disks used for stori computer programs and information are called disks or diskettes. Most disk uni for home computer systems take flexibl 'floppy' disks, 13.3 cm (5¼ in) in diamete or smaller, rigid disks.

Dot matrix An arrangement of dots fr which various combinations are used to print individual letters, numerals and other characters.

Graphics Pictures or diagrams display on the computer screen or made on pap

ieans of a printer or plotter.

d copy Text, figures or graphics from
nputer that have been printed or
ed on paper.

dware The equipment used to make
 computer system.

stick A control stick used instead of
keyboard, usually for playing
outer games.

te A unit for measuring the size of a
outer's memory. One Kbyte is equal
)24 bytes.

it pen A pen-shaped device that can
sed for drawing pictures on the
outer screen. When the pen touches
screen it sends signals to the
outer that indicate which part of the
en it is on. The computer can respond
ediately by illuminating that spot on
screen, so it appears as if the pen is
king it. The pen can also be used for
r purposes, such as selecting the
ver to a question from a list of words
vn on the screen. As the computer
vs where the pen is, it knows which
l has been selected.

nframe A large computer system of
type used by businesses, such as
ks and insurance companies.

nory The part of a computer that
es information and programs.

roprocessor A chip containing a
ly complex circuit that controls the
ation of a computer.

lem A device used for linking a
outer to a telephone line to enable
munication with other computers. The
em changes computer signals into a
l that can be sent through the
ohone system. It also changes signals
ived via the telephone system into the
l required by the computer. The two
esses used to convert the signals are
d *mo*dulation and *dem*odulation.

iitor A unit used instead of a
vision set for displaying the words and
ires from a computer.

ise A device, about the size of a
se, attached to the computer by a
 (the 'tail'), used to move a cursor or
e other object around the screen.
en the mouse is moved by hand over a
surface it sends signals to the
outer to make a similar movement on
screen.

Pixel A picture element – the smallest
area of the screen that can be individually
controlled when forming pictures. It
would take a large amount of memory to
store information about the colour and
brightness of each dot on the screen, so
the dots are usually controlled in groups.

Plotter A device for drawing pictures and
characters according to commands sent
from a computer.

Program A set of instructions written in
a computer language, such as BASIC. The
program determines what task the
computer performs.

RAM Random Access Memory, the part
of the computer's memory where programs
and information are temporarily stored.

ROM Read Only Memory, the computer's
permanent store of information that it
needs in order to operate. One part of the
ROM, for example, stores information on
how to form characters on the screen.

Simulation Using a computer to
demonstrate the way something behaves
or appears. An image on the screen is
made to act or look like a real object. For
example, you could see how a ball would
bounce when dropped from various
heights onto different surfaces.

Software Another name for the
programs that tell a computer what to do.

Sprite A graphics image that can easily
be moved around the screen.

Synthesizer An electronic device for
making music or sounds like the human
voice. A music synthesizer is usually
fitted with a piano-style keyboard. A voice
or speech synthesizer may consist of a
separate unit that is connected to the
computer. Or it may simply be a chip that
can be plugged permanently into a spare
socket inside the computer.

Tracker ball A control device used to
move objects around the screen. The ball
protrudes from a box and can be turned in
any direction with the fingers. The
movement generates signals, which cause
an object on the screen to move in the
same direction.

Turtle A mobile robot that can draw as it
moves around on the floor. Also a cursor
that draws on the screen as it moves.

Word processing The use of computer
equipment to write, edit or print letters or
other documents.

INDEX

3-D graphics 21
Acoustic coupler 45
Advanced Music
    System 38
Adventure games 19
Aerobatics 21
American Express 47
Amstrad PCW 8256 24
Analogue signals 36
Animation 30–31
Apricot F1 43
Arcades 19
Atari 21

BASIC examples 14–15
Bar codes 53
Binary system 10, 32
Bits 10
Blind people, aids for
    50–51
Block graphics 29, 30,
    32
Braille link 50–51
Bulletin Board
    Systems (BBS) 45–
    46
Bushnell, Nolan 19
Business
    communications 45
Bytes 10

Cars 40
Cartoons 21
Cassette recorder 9
Chips 10
Commodore 64 31, 38
Communicating with
    computers 40–51
Concept keyboards 51

Daisy wheel printer
    26–27
Databases 47–48
Deaf people, aids for 50
Digigraph 34
Digital sounds 36
Digitizers 32
Disk drive 25

Disk unit 9
Dot matrix printer 27

Electronic clocks 40
Electronic paintbox 34–
    35
Entertaining computers
    18–21

Factories 54–60
Fairlight 36
Firebird Software 38
Flight simulators 22–23
FORTH 14, 15

Games 18–21, 40, 48–49
Graetz, Martin 18
Grand Prix racing 21
Graphics
    animation 30–31
    block 29, 30, 32
    electronic paintbox
      34–35
    games 18, 21
    light pens 34
    made easy 32–35
    paper, on 35
    simple 29
    sprites 30, 31
    tablets 32
    uses 28

Handicapped people,
    help for 50–51
Hard copy 26
Hardware 9
Home computers 9, 19,
    38

Information services 44,
    47–48, 50
Inside computers 10–11
Instructions, vital 14–15

Joystick unit 9, 22

Keyboards 51
Koala-pad 32–33

Light pens 34

LISP 16
LOGO 15

Mainframe computers
    18
Massachusetts Institute
    of Technology 18
Memories 9, 10–11
Microprocessor 10
Microwriter 25
Mobile robots 60
Modem 45, 46
Monitor 25
Music
    home micro 38
    making 36–38
    processing 37
    sampling 37
    sequencers 36, 37
    studio sounds 36–37
    synthesizers 36–37
My Talking Computer
    40

Namal Type & Talk
    unit 42

Opticon 51

Pairs of printed pictures
    21
Penman Plotter 34
Pens, light 34
People Mover 60
Phonemes 41
Photonic wand 50, 51
Plotter 35
Pong 18, 19, 21
Printer
    daisy wheel 26–27
    dot matrix 27, 35
Private communications
    45–46
Program
    examples of BASIC
      14–15
    loading 9
    user friendliness 16

Random Access Memory
    (RAM) 10, 11, 42
Read And write Memory
    see Random Access
    Memory

Read Only Memory
    (ROM) 10–11, 42
Robots
    arms 54, 58–59
    assembly 58
    gripping device 58
    handling device 58
    holding parts 59
    on the move 60
    pick and place 58
    uses 54
Roland GR700 37
Running programs 15

Sales of computers
    boom 6–7
    crash 7
    problems 7
Sampling 37
Sensors 60
Sentence Maker 41
Sequencers 36, 37
Shops 52–53
Simulations 21–23
Software 9
Source, The 48
Space invaders 18, 19
Spacewar 18
Speak 'n' Spell 40
Speech
    recognition 43
    synthesis 40, 41, 44,
      50
Sprites 30, 31
Supermarkets 52, 53
Switch system 51
Synclavier 36
Synth-Axe 37
Synthesizers 36–37, 40,
    41, 44, 50

Tablets
    digitizing 32
    graphics 32
Talkative robots 60
Talking Calculator 41
Talking computers 40
Talking Story 41
Telephones 44–45, 50
Telling the Time 41
Texas Instruments 40
Text by telephone 44, 45
Turtles in classroom 60

Ultrasonics 60
User friendliness 16
Using computers
    home computer
      equipment 9
    other hardware 9

Valhalla 20
Videotext 44
Viewdata service 4
Vizaspell 25
Vizawrite 25
Voicemate 43

Westinghouse
    Corporation 6(
Word processing 9,
    26
Word stores 42

Yamaha CX5M 35

Zapping aliens 19
Zeaker 54

Acknowledgeme

A.B. European
Marketing Division
Photo Agency, Ata
B.B.C., J. Berton-(
State University, I
Telecom, Michael
Connolly/Scripps (
Ian Dobbie, Educa
Computing Magaz
Ford Motor Compa
Liz Heaney, Dr.
Johannes Heidenh
Ellis Herwig, Dav
Higham, Roy Ingra
Ralph Jessop Ltd,
Lodge, Ian Mckinr
Newcastle Polytec
Popperfoto, Preste
Ruffler and Deith
Science Photo Libr
Siggraph, Spectrur
Colour Library, Ch
Stevens, Tony Sto
Worldwide, Crispi
Thomas, Marcus V
Smith.